Gresley
Locomotives

Gresley Locomotives

A Pictorial History by Brian Haresnape

IAN ALLAN Publishing

Contents

First published 1981
Reprinted 1993

ISBN 0 7110 0892 2

Published by Ian Allan Ltd,
Shepperton, Surrey; and printed by
Ian Allan Printing Ltd at its works at
Coombelands in Runnymede, England.

Introduction

When Geoffrey Freeman Allen, then Editorial Director of Ian Allan Ltd, first discussed the idea of a series of pictorial histories of the locomotives of leading British steam engineers with me, back in 1968, the name Gresley was one of the first to spring to mind. We both agreed that a good deal of attention had already been paid to Gresley's engines, but that scope existed to produce a further work. Scope indeed, as it has turned out! In fact one volume barely provides enough space to cover the tremendous achievements of this one man's career. Few people have the honour of becoming legends in their own lifetime (fewer still probably deserve it) but this is exactly what Gresley became, and in no uncertain way. His following was both wide and devoted, and the achievements of his locomotives were the pride of the British public.

As a young man I was presented one Christmas with a slender volume, printed to wartime economy standards, entitled *The Locomotives of Sir Nigel Gresley*, by O. S. Nock. This was my introduction to Gresley's fine machines; just at the end of World War 2. Of course, having read about them one simply had to see them! We lived at that time close to the LMSR main line at Kenton in Middlesex, and my only glimpses of LNER steam had been snatched from an overbridge at nearby Harrow-on-the-Hill, where Marylebone line trains intermingled with London Transport's ceaseless electrics. Compared to the grimy majesty of the Euston main line, these Great Central line descendants seemed thin and ephemeral. Dare one say it – rather like a superior branch line!

The day of discovery was to come quite soon. A trip to Kings Cross to say farewell to a relative, late on a misty September afternoon (or was the mist just smoke!) immediately revealed the true splendours of LNER steam. In 1947 the postwar colours of garter blue and apple green were just beginning to make their appearance amidst the overall dirty black of wartime, and in that curious murk that always clung to the interior of the Kings Cross trainshed in steam days, I was immensely impressed by the line-up of Pacifics at the buffer stops. Pride of place of course was taken by a recently outshopped 'A4' with polished stainless steel letters and numerals upon a garter blue finish and with those elegant wheels glistening in an oily Indian red. My eye was captured by this sight, and soon my ear was to rejoice in the melodious tones of the engine's chime whistle. Here was something I had previously seen only in cast-metal toys of crude finish, and in my cherished book by Nock, where such engines were shown streaking past the camera in black and white

pictures, at the head of prewar streamliners. This particular locomotive was adorned by a decorative motif which even my mother, normally unmoved by steam trains, paused to admire – it depicted a Silver Fox. Here was one of Gresley's masterpieces! From that day on visits to Kings Cross became part of many a day's outing to London, and remained so until the very end of steam.

Of course it was not long before the appeal of other Gresley types made its mark on me, and the graceful 'A3s' in particular captivated my eye. In 1948-9 the newly nationalised railway system was still in the throes of all manner of administrative upheavals, and much of the previous LNER identity remained unchanged, although I well recall the shock of seeing some of the 'A3s' painted in blue. At first they tried out a very dark ultramarine shade (like the old Great Eastern Railway livery), and then a brighter Caledonian blue, with black and white lining. It simply did not suit them, although the streamlined 'A4s' carried it quite well. It's strange how certain locomotive types only look their best in certain colours. In the case of the 'A3s' it was the LNER apple green; even the BR Brunswick green shade looked wrong by comparison.

If my own enthusiasm for Gresley's locomotives was initially sparked-off by their *appearance,* then I suppose I was not alone, because they certainly had style and good looks. But many enthusiasts were equally motivated by their *performance* on the road. I must confess that I had no chance to sample this until the early 1950s, when 'spotting' trips to Doncaster and York were to reveal the true delights of LNER main line running. Actually my first recorded trip behind a Gresley engine was a miserable affair indeed! This was on the 'Norfolk-man' between Ipswich and Liverpool Street in 1951, and the train engine was his pioneer three-cylinder Class B17 4-6-0 No 61600 *Sandringham.* In pouring rain and with the engine in quite obviously run-down state we lost time steadily on a duty normally worked at that time by one of the new Standard 'Britannia' Pacifics. This run introduced me to one of the less attractive aspects of Gresley's designs; namely that they did not respond well to neglect. Whereas, for example, a Stanier engine could get rough as mileage was clocked-up, but could still respond willingly when flogged, the more sophisticated Gresley types were sometimes sad to encounter. Like a good horse they needed to be well groomed, well fed and well shod – and *then* how they could run!

The object of this book is to present in pictorial form all the locomotive types which are attributed to this great engineer. The emphasis is upon the various detail alterations made to various types over the years that they were in service, and I have selected illustrations to emphasise these points, as they are of particular interest to railway modellers. The book reveals quite neatly the two phases of

Above: Class A3 Pacific No 60080 *Dick Turpin* heads for York out of Newcastle Central, hauling an Edinburgh-Kings Cross express on 9 April 1955. *Ian Allan Library*

Right: Front rank express power of the Ivatt regime were the classic Atlantics with wide firebox and big boiler. Gresley further improved the design with the use of superheating and in some cases the fitting of piston valves instead of slide-valves. The 4-4-2s were then capable of some brilliant running for engines of this size and weight. Nos 3296 and 3291 are seen double-heading the 1.40pm King Cross-Harrogate express, some time in 1930. The increasingly heavy loads which necessitated such double-heading led Gresley to formulate his 'big engine' policy. *F. R. Hebron*

Gresley's long and distinguished career. In the first phase we see the products of his formative years, when he inherited the practices of Stirling and Ivatt on the Great Northern Railway, and began to graft his own ideas upon the stolid Doncaster tradition, leading up to his 'big engine' policy. In the second phase, we see the later stages of this well-known 'big engine' policy, culminating with the era of the streamliners.

A brief biographical note is all I wish to contribute on the subject of Gresley the man, as this book is essentially about his engines. Some excellent studies have been written about Gresley, and these are listed in the Bibliography on page 176.

Herbert Nigel Gresley was born in Edinburgh on 19 June 1876. His father was the Rev Nigel Gresley, who had been born at Netherseale Hall, Derbyshire, the ninth of the Gresley Baronets. A quiet childhood at the Rectory was followed by preparatory school at St Leonards-on-Sea from the age of eight until fourteen, when he went to Marlborough College for three years, proving to be an average rather than an outstanding scholar. Leaving Marlborough, Gresley chose a railway career, and went first to the Crewe Works of the London & North Western Railway where he served under the formidable F. W. Webb as a premium apprentice. His time at Crewe was well spent; it even included a year working in the fitting and erecting shops. A desire to obtain drawing office experience led to a move from Crewe to Horwich, where the Lancashire & Yorkshire Railway had recently opened its new workshop. At Horwich Gresley served under Mr (later Sir) J. A. F. Aspinall and that notable locomotive engineer designed and built his large-boilered inside cylinder Atlantics while Gresley was there. Having gained some experience as a draughtsman, he was then placed in charge of the Horwich Materials Test Room for a while, before being sent to the important and strenuous task of Foreman of Blackpool locomotive sheds. This must have opened Gresley's eyes to the many difficulties of day-to-day locomotive operations, because Blackpool was an extremely busy shed, particularly during the holiday season.

Gresley's attentions were now to switch to carriages and rolling stock, rather than locomotives, and this move was to have considerable beneficial

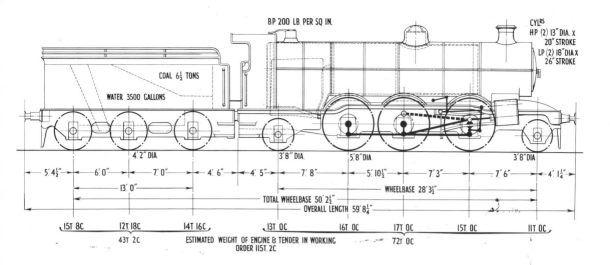

BP 200 LB. PER SQ IN.

CYL^{RS}
HP (2) 13" DIA. X 20" STROKE
LP (2) 18" DIA X 26" STROKE

COAL 6½ TONS

WATER 3500 GALLONS

4' 2" DIA.   3' 8" DIA.   5' 8" DIA   3' 8" DIA

5' 4½" — 6' 0" — 7' 0" — 4' 6" — 4' 5" — 7' 8" — 5' 10½" — 7' 3" — 7' 6" — 4' 1¼"

13' 0"   WHEELBASE 28' 3½"

TOTAL WHEELBASE 50' 2½"
OVERALL LENGTH 59' 8¼"

15T 8C   12T 18C   14T 16C   13T 0C   16T 0C   17T 0C   15T 0C   11T 0C

43T 2C   ESTIMATED WEIGHT OF ENGINE & TENDER IN WORKING   72T 0C
              ORDER 115T. 2C

influence upon his later career. He was first of all appointed Outdoor Assistant to the LYR Carriage & Wagon Superintendent, and then in 1901 (aged 25) was appointed to be Assistant Works Manager at the Newton Heath Carriage & Wagon works (incidentally getting married the same year). Three years later he was promoted to the post of Assistant Superintendent at Newton Heath.

In 1905, by which time Gresley had two small children, he moved to Doncaster, to take up the post of Superintendent of the Great Northern Railways' Carriage & Wagon Department. Gresley's activities as a rolling stock engineer, which were to continue for the rest of his life, are outside the scope of our present story, but it is proper to acknowledge this aspect of his work in passing. He produced some of the most superb carriages ever to run on any railway in Britain, or indeed in the world, and he developed specific aspects, such as bogie design, to a refined art. So successful in fact was his double-bolster bogie design that even in the 1950s British Railways reverted to it in preference to BR's own single-bolster bogie design (which had proved to be rough-riding) for some new electric multiple-unit stock. Readers who wish to learn more about this side of Gresley's activities are referred to the paper presented by N. Newsome to the Institution of Locomotive Engineers in 1948. It can truly be said that Gresley designed *trains* rather than just locomotives, and that the passenger benefitted from this complete achievement.

Gresley took time to implement his own ideas. Some of these undoubtedly resulted from his study of contemporary British and American practice and some were the product of original thinking. Boilers were to get steadily bigger, and the number of cylinders was to be decided from experience. On the Great Western Railway G. J. Churchward was already showing the way to future British steam locomotive design, and in 1903 and 1905 he had

Above: By about 1907, the need for a larger type of locomotive, to work the developing fast goods traffic, led Ivatt to consider the design of a large mixed traffic 2-6-2, with an Atlantic-type boiler and wide firebox, and four compound cylinders. Although this graceful engine never passed the drawing board stage it foreshadowed in some respects Gresley's fine 'V2' 2-6-2 design of later years.

even gone to the lengths of importing some French De Glehn-Du Bousqet four-cylinder compound Atlantics in order to assess their performance. Gresley, at that time involved with carriage and wagon affairs, nevertheless must have watched this development with considerable interest, because the Great Northern was then producing Atlantic locomotives, to the designs of H. A. Ivatt, as its prime express passenger type. Significantly the GNR ordered a four-cylinder Atlantic, based upon French practice, from Vulcan Foundry, for comparative trials with Ivatt's designs, in 1905. Other types that Churchward produced included a 2-8-0 two-cylinder heavy freight locomotive, the '2800' class of 1903, some smaller designs for standard tank engines and then his four-cylinder 4-6-0 'Star' class in 1906. The attentions of the men of the locomotive world were constantly focused upon the exploits of Swindon under Churchward, and this attention came to a climax in 1908 when the first British Pacific, No 111 *The Great Bear* was revealed to an astonished public. At a time when many British lines relied upon modest inside-cylinder 0-6-0s and 0-8-0s for goods traffic, and medium sized 4-4-0s, 4-6-0s or Atlantics for passenger work, the products of Swindon were a revelation. Gresley, still a young man, cannot have failed to be impressed by what Churchward was achieving, and he would have read about his designs in the learned journals of the day, which described them in great detail. Similarly the contemporary American developments were well chronicled, with their advances in boiler design and improved valve gear.

In 1911 H. A. Ivatt retired from GNR service, and the Directors appointed H. N. Gresley to the post of Locomotive Engineer; on 1 October to be precise. At the age of 35 he commenced a task which was to see him active and forceful for the next 30 years. An important partnership for the years ahead was now to take place. This was the appointment in January 1912, as his personal assistant, of O. V. S. Bulleid. Having commenced an apprenticeship under H. A. Ivatt, at Doncaster in 1901 Bulleid had gone to work in Europe in 1907, but returned to the GNR in December 1911.

Under Ivatt the GNR locomotive affairs had progressed from the 4-2-2 era of Stirling to the 4-4-2, without superheater. By 1911, when in October, H. N. Gresley was appointed to the post of Locomotive Superintendent of the GNR, the mainly saturated Ivatt Atlantics were working hard, but not always brilliantly, and they were even to be found on fast goods work. Such work was not really suited to a 4-4-2 layout, but there was a boom in fast goods traffic business for which the GNR did not possess any really suitable engines. Ivatt had a superheated 0-6-0 goods engine with 5ft 2in-diameter wheels on the drawing board and Gresley completed these, with an initial batch of 15 in 1911, known as the '536' class. Presumably to achieve faster running, Gresley then produced a superheated 0-6-0 with 5ft 8in diameter wheels, capable of taking a train up to a mile-a-minute. Ten of these, Nos 71–80, were employed on through goods trains between York and London as well as some passenger work, and they proved to be very successful engines.

These 0-6-0s represent the last of Ivatt's designs rather than the first of Gresley's. In fact in 1907 Ivatt had considered a four-cylinder compound 2-6-2 mixed-traffic design, suitable for fast goods work, but this did not get beyond the drawing board stage. This engine would have had his large Atlantic boiler and firebox, and 5ft 8in driving wheels. But by the time Gresley came to consider an engine larger than the latest 0-6-0s, for mixed-traffic use, the 2-6-0, or Mogul, wheel arrangement had become firmly established by Churchward, with his '4300' class of 1911. Gresley's first locomotive design was to be a Mogul, the GNR Class H2 (LNER Class K1) of 1912, and 10 were built. The main advance was in their front end layout, which featured two outside cylinders and Walschaerts valve gear, with the running plate raised high over the wheels. They were somewhat under-boilered for their cylinder dimensions, but they soon revealed a capacity for hard work, particularly during the exceptional traffic demands of World War 1.

Drawing office practice tends to dictate solutions to the lesser elements of railway designs. Hence, for example, there were usually ready-made drawing office solutions to the design of the cab, of footsteps, grab rails, shape of chimney and many other details which, at first, Gresley was willing to accept. Indeed the complete tender design of the Ivatt period sufficed to begin with. Gresley was grappling with more fundamental problems. This accounts for the odd combination of modern outside Walschaerts valve gear and a pony truck put together with the somewhat primitive Ivatt cum-Stirling cab which was a feature of Gresley's first Mogul design. Even the early Pacific proposals featured a cab without side windows, but fortunately by the time the famous pioneer Gresley Pacifics arrived upon the scene in 1922, these aspects of locomotive design had received renewed attention at Doncaster, with the result that a truly fine machine took the rails—modern in every respect.

The Mogul was a step in the right direction for the fast freights, and once Gresley increased the size of the boiler, in 1914, when the first of the 'E1' class (LNER 'K2') appeared, then the company possessed an excellent mixed-traffic machine. But the massive coal trains which ran between Peterborough and London, worked by Ivatt's 'Long Tom' Class 401 0-8-0s, had grown to such proportions by 1912/3

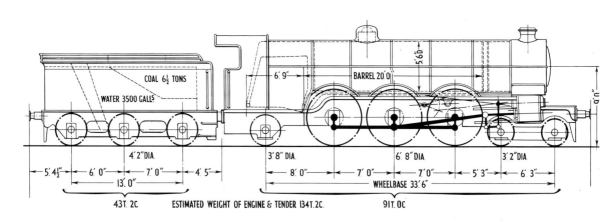

Top left: Superheated 0-6-0 design, with 5ft 8in diameter wheels, of basically Ivatt inspiration, produced by Gresley for fast freight work in 1912. Ten were constructed, Nos 71-80, and No 73 is seen here in full GNR green livery; later known as the 'J2' class. *W. J. Reynolds*

Centre left: In July 1905 the GNR had taken delivery from Vulcan Foundry of a four-cylinder compound Atlantic, based on De Glehn practice. Gresley rebuilt the engine, No 1300, as a two-cylinder simple in 1917, using the standard 20in by 26in outside cylinders of his Moguls (GNR Classes H2 and H3,) because the original cylinders required replacement. The original boiler and long shallow firebox were retained, with working pressure reduced from 200lb per sq in to 170lb per sq in and a new standard pattern smokebox was fitted, with outside steampipes to the cylinders. *A. B. MacLeod Collection*

Bottom left: The 1915 proposal for a four-cylinder Pacific, with the wide firebox and large boiler introduced by Ivatt for his Atlantics, married to a front end based upon current GWR practice. The working pressure would have been 170lb per sq in and the four cylinders were 15in by 26in. In the same year Gresley designed and patented two designs of conjugated valve gear for use with three-cylinder engines, although three years elapsed before an engine was constructed embodying the gear (see page 10).

Below: The pioneer Gresley Pacific design taking shape, with a three-cylinder layout, but retaining at this stage a traditional Doncaster cab and six-wheeled tender. The original drawing was produced in 1920.

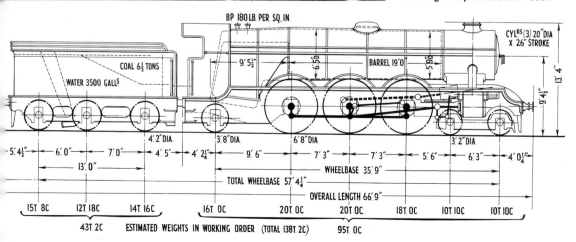

9

Above: Class A1 Pacific No 4474 *Victor Wild* seen departing from Kings Cross with the down 'Norseman', 13 June 1931 with the new all-electric signalbox under construction behind the engine. The engine was by this time fitted with long-travel valve gear, following the results of the comparative trials with Collett's GWR 'Castle' class 4-6-0s. *Ian Allan Library*

that Gresley had to produce a new 2-8-0 design, the '456' (LNER Class 01), with two outside cylinders and Walschaerts valve gear. Like the Moguls this was a very straightforward design, and certain traditional Doncaster features were retained.

If Gresley's first engines were of the two-cylinder type, this was in all probability dictated by the types of traffic they were intended for, rather than by any particular preference for this arrangement on Gresley's part. Elsewhere in Britain compound and multi-cylindered engines were appearing, and the application of superheating was gaining widespread approval. We have already seen Churchward's pioneer work leading to his standard four-cylinder simple expansion machines of great power and efficiency. Ivatt had made some tentative experiments with four cylinders and with compound working and superheating, and Gresley would have had ample chance to study these. In 1915 he selected an Ivatt Atlantic, No 279, for rebuilding as a four-cylinder simple, at the same time fitting it with a larger 24-element Robinson superheater. Wartime conditions were probably the main reason for lack of further developments of this type (one or two other rebuildings excepted), until May 1918 when his first three-cylinder engine appeared. This was the 2-8-0 No 461, which had an identical boiler to the two-cylinder '456' class, but providing steam for a front end having three cylinders arranged in line; of which more anon.

In retrospect it seems that during the period 1914-18, while the Great War raged in Europe, Gresley and his staff were busy pondering upon the future locomotive needs of the company. Wartime traffic was stretching the performances of existing locomotives to the very limits, and it must have been abundantly clear that for passenger work a larger locomotive, possibly of the Pacific type, would be required. Ivatt's wide firebox and large boiler could be married to a Churchward type four-cylinder layout, in Gresley's view (hence the experiment with No 279 already mentioned) and drawings were prepared showing first a Prairie and then a Pacific proposal along these lines. From this, and with experience of No 279 in traffic, Gresley progressed to the idea of using only three cylinders, worked by a form of conjugated valve gear, which would avoid the need for three complete sets of valve gear and would operate the valves of the middle cylinder. Designs for the 2-8-0, No 461, were completed in 1916, but due to the war the engine could not be constructed for a further two years. Gresley borrowed the GWR Swindon dynamometer car from Churchward, in order to test No 461 once it was on the road, and was so impressed by the performance that he resolved to apply the three-cylinder layout to all his future engines.

The form of conjugated valve gear devised by Gresley and applied to No 461, with the three cylinders steeply inclined at an angle of 1 in 8 (in order to avoid the inside crosshead fouling the leading coupled axle), met with some informed criticism in the technical press. One outcome of this was the now legendary meeting at Kings Cross in January 1919, following some correspondence, between Gresley and H. Holcroft. Whilst working at Swindon, Holcroft had devised a more refined form

Above: Sir Vincent Raven's Pacific design for the North Eastern Railway, which Gresley compared with his own Pacifics in 1923, was an imposing machine but somewhat dated in its front end concept. Gresley took No 2404 *City of Ripon* and reboilered it with an 'A1' boiler in an attempt to improve steaming and performance, at the same time adding his own cab design. The engine ran coupled to a Gresley eight-wheel tender for a period as seen here. Gresley even considered fitting an 'A3' boiler in 1933, but this did not happen and the Raven Pacifics were withdrawn from service during the 1936/7 period when their boilers became due for renewal. Despite being less successful than the Gresley design, they put in considerable hard work in their final years when based at York. *P. Ransome-Wallis*

Right: For service in Scotland Gresley ordered some Robinson Great Central 'Improved Director' 4-4-0s, having earlier sent some Ivatt engines to the area. In early BR days No 2691 *Laird of Balmawhapple* in LNER apple green livery, but lettered 'British Railways' on the tender, is seen bustling along on a passenger train. The boiler mountings had to be cut down to suit the Scottish loading gauge, so the engines lacked the graceful Robinson chimney. *E. R. Wethersett*

of conjugated valve gear for three cylinders, and had taken this with him to Ashford, where he was then working under R. E. L. Maunsell. Gresley was so impressed by Holcroft's design that he wanted to use it immediately, and he also tried without success to persuade Maunsell to release Holcroft, so that the latter could go to work for him at Doncaster. The Doncaster drawing office was now busy scheming a number of designs using the three-cylinder layout.

An important development occurred at the end of 1918 when Gresley proceeded to superheat all the Ivatt Atlantics. Following experiments with No 1403, which was given new cylinders and piston valves,

and a 32-element Robinson superheater, all the large Atlantics were superheated by 1934, with impressive effect upon their abilities to run and upon their coal and water consumption.

By 1919 Gresley was well settled in at Doncaster. In his private life he now had four children, and at work he once again had O.V.S. Bulleid as his personal assistant, following Bulleid's return from war service. With the return to peacetime there were new problems to face, with a coal strike, raw material shortages and the possibility of an amalgamation of the railway companies, which in August 1921 were returned to their prewar owners by the Government, which had taken control of them during the war.

The first three-cylinder 2-6-0 appeared in March 1920, and a singularly impressive looking machine it turned out to be! The big boiler, no less than 6ft in diameter, meant that only a small chimney and dome could be accommodated within the loading

Above: Gresley took another Robinson Great Central Railway design, an 0-8-4T shunting tank for Wath hump marshalling yard, and developed it. These three-cylinder engines were being worked to capacity, so Gresley fitted one with a superheated boiler and a reversible booster on the trailing bogie, with the wheels coupled. Two new engines, No 2798/9, were then built to the same design, except for a cutaway front to the side tanks to improve forward vision. Appendix 1 gives details of the various modifications Gresley made to existing designs in his quest for improvement. *British Rail*

gauge and this gave a very modern look to the engine, although retention of the old style GNR cab, without side windows, slightly marred the effect. Like the previous Gresley two-cylinder Moguls, the new type proved to be rather lively riders, especially at speed, but in all other respects the engines quickly shone and were much respected for their performance. A natural follow-up was the production of a three-cylinder version of the large 2-8-0 design, using the more refined form of conjugated valve gear with Holcroft's modifications and as a result these were of more conventional modern appearance than the prototype No 461 had been.

Secrecy seems to have surrounded the final design stages and then construction of Gresley's first Pacific. Rumour had been strong whilst the big three-cylinder Mogul was being built that it was in fact something even grander; but of course its subsequent appearance scotched this. Then, as F.A.S. Brown has recalled in his book *From Stirling to Gresley* (Oxford Publishing Co), these persistant rumours next seemed to be confirmed by the decision, taken in October 1920, to install a new 70ft turntable at Grantham. The existing turntable could only just accommodate an Atlantic, so surely there must be something bigger on its way? Indeed there was, for drawings were just being completed for the three-cylinder Pacific which had been exercising Gresley's mind since the war years.

It was perhaps fitting that the first two of Gresley's fabled Pacifics, Nos 1470/1, should appear on the scene in the closing days of the Great Northern Railway, in 1922. The following January was to see the GNR absorbed as one of the constituents of the mighty London & North Eastern Railway, and subsequent LNER locomotive history was to involve many influences from beyond Doncaster, as we shall shortly see. But the first two Gresley Pacifics proudly sported the livery of the GNR when first delivered and as if to add emphasis to the achievement, No 1470 was named *Great Northern*. Comparison with Britain's first Pacific design, Churchward's *The Great Bear,* showed that Gresley was in most respects considerably advancing the art of the locomotive. They were certainly fine looking machines, and the modern side-window cab and eight-wheeled tender was a great advance upon previous Doncaster practice. It of course remained to be seen if they could perform as handsomely on the road, and happily this aspect was soon demonstrated so convincingly that a further 10 locomotives were ordered by the GNR, although these were delivered under LNER auspices.

Another Pacific design now appeared on the scene, by Sir Vincent Raven for the North Eastern Railway. Here again amalgamation intervened and the NER became a part of the LNER group just as they were delivered. So it was that the rival design was now owned by the same group. Naturally the LNER wanted to compare the two Pacific designs, with an eye to the future needs of the new company. With the amalgamation, Nigel Gresley had been selected by the Board of the newly formed LNER to become their Chief Mechanical Engineer, and he had moved his headquarters office to Kings Cross station; putting his family in a house in Hertfordshire. Gresley soon compared the Raven Pacific against his own, by bringing about a series of trials whereby the NER design worked north from Kings

Left: Gresley was a firm believer in 'horses for courses' and during his regime both the Great Central and the Great Eastern areas largely retained their locomotive stock, with little Doncaster infiltration. He did however regard it as necessary to effect some improvements to the existing engines, as in the case of the inside-cylinder 'B12' 4-6-0s where he fitted new boilers of his design, and introduced an improved front end; these changes resulted in a marked improvement in performance. No 61553 is seen here near Corby Glen with a Grantham-Peterborough local train in April 1956. *P. H. Groom*

Right: Three tank engine proposals that did not materialise: a 3-cylinder 0-8-0T for shunting use, a 3-cylinder 2-6-4T specifically intended for the Great Northern section London surburban services, and a 3-cylinder 2-8-2T intended for local mineral working.

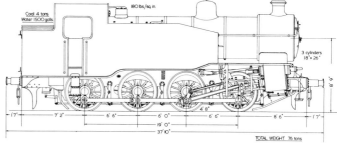

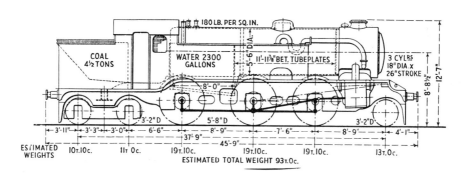

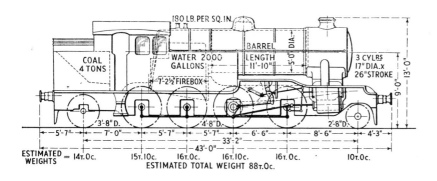

Right: The problem of smoke and steam obscuring the driver's vision is well demonstrated in this picture of Class P2 Mikado No 2002 *Earl Marischal* at speed on the East Coast main line. This particular engine, with Walschaerts valve gear, was more prone to this trouble than No 2001 *Cock o' the North,* which had poppet valves and a fiercer exhaust. *C. C. B. Herbert*

Cross, over former GNR metals. The Raven design was in reality an outgrown, stretched version of his classic NER 'Z' class superheated Atlantics, and in many respects it lacked the modern approach of Gresley, particularly in respect of front end layout and valve gear, and it soon proved to be an indifferent steamer. Later (in 1929), Gresley fitted a new boiler to one engine, see page 11, in an attempt to improve steaming and performance, but no great advantage resulted and the Raven Pacifics did not last very long after that. Their fate had been sealed when the LNER ordered a further 40 of the Gresley engines, as a result of these comparative trials.

Notwithstanding their initial success, the first Gresley Pacifics were to meet their match in some further trials, with important effects upon their future. In July 1923 the Great Western Railway proudly unveiled the first of C.B. Collett's 'Castle' class four-cylinder 4-6-0s, No 4073 *Caerphilly Castle,* which with a tractive effort of 31,625lb, some 2,000lb more than either LNER Pacific design, allowed the GWR to claim them as Britain's most powerful express locomotives. To add salt to the wound, *Caerphilly Castle* was exhibited in the Palace of Engineering at the British Empire Exhibition at Wembley in 1924. Close-by was Gresley's Pacific No 4472 specially named *Flying Scotsman.* Was the smaller 4-6-0 really more powerful than the graceful larger Pacific? The public, especially the enthusiasts of the day, were keen to know, and they were soon to be given the answer. The exploits of the GWR engine No 4079 *Pendennis Castle* in trial running on the LNER main line showed conclusively that the Churchward-inspired front end layout, with long-travel valves, and the higher boiler pressure, made the 4-6-0 a freer-running engine than the Pacifics. As a result Gresley began experiments with long-travel valves, and these showed a considerable improvement in the Pacifics' running, as well as economising in coal consumption. The whole class was gradually altered, with a very beneficial effect.

The creation of the LNER brought together six major railway companies. To Gresley fell the task of providing suitable new motive power and improving the existing stock where this could be done. He was a firm believer in 'horses for courses' and he took advice from his four Area Mechanical Engineers. Why, he argued, should he design and build entirely new types of engine if existing designs would suffice? Perhaps they could be improved in some respects, but the latest products of the pre-Grouping companies were in some cases very admirable designs, well suited to the areas they had been built to serve. Indeed the Great Eastern and Great Central areas retained their own stock for many years, with very little Doncaster influence apparent. Gresley even ordered Robinson's Great Central Railway 'Improved Director' 4-4-0s for service in Scotland, and he continued to build the Hill 0-6-2T Class N7 of Great Eastern origin, with later examples from Doncaster having his round-topped fireboxes. Boilers of Gresley design were later to be fitted to other former Great Eastern classes, and Gresley subjected some pre-Grouping engine designs to various trials with poppet valves, feedwater heaters and boosters. Significantly this great locomotive engineer did not attempt to flood the LNER with Doncaster-inspired designs, unlike

the sad story of the LMSR during the same period, when everyone knew that Derby ruled!

So far we have seen how Gresley established himself as an extremely able engineer. The artist in him had begun to show in the shapely lines of his three-cylinder Moguls and in the Pacifics, and with these a Gresley 'style' had emerged, more feminine in its curvature, perhaps, than the masculine Churchward would have accepted! The choice by the LNER Board of apple green livery for the larger engines must have pleased him—reminding him of his GNR days—and it must be said that it admirably complemented his designs (except when tried out on the streamlined 'A4s'). It has been observed that there were some strange 'hallmarks' to his designs. One was the tendency for the valve motion to make a clanking sound when in movement, a phenomenon first observed in the 2-6-0s; another was the distinctive exhaust beat of the three-cylinder layout. This beat could be quite unnerving if the engine concerned was overdue for shopping and attention to valve settings.

Gresley sought standardisation wherever possible, but never simply for its own sake, and he did not hesitate to try out various alternatives to the Gresley/Holcroft three-cylinder conjugated valve gear. By the mid-1920s the Gresley locomotive stud was multiplying, with more 'K3' Moguls and with the follow-on order for Pacifics. At this time a need arose for more of the humble and faithful 0-6-0 goods engines, for lesser duties. Gresley decided to pursue his own big engine policy in this area as well. He first of all produced 35 very large 0-6-0 mineral engines for the North British section, to meet an urgent need. These, the 'J38' class, had 4ft 8in

diameter coupled wheels well suited to their duties, but he followed on with a revised version, the 'J39' class, with 5ft 2in coupled wheels and more of a mixed-traffic type. These later engines were quite remarkable examples of their type, able to haul good loads of passengers or freight, with excellent acceleration, and they were very free running at high speeds. Indeed, so successful was this design that batches were built year by year until no less than 289 had been delivered, and they had become a familiar sight on the widespread LNER system.

However, before these 0-6-0s appeared, Gresley had produced some very large freight locomotives. His two impressive Class P1 Mikados of 1925 were a logical freight version of his Pacific design and were intended for the heavy mineral traffic carried over the GN main line. Their 'Achilles heel' was to prove to be their ability to handle immense loads of 100 wagons, totalling some 1,600 tons. These were easily handled by these locos, but disposing of them in the existing refuge loops and sidings was another story!

At about the same time one of the most remarkable steam locomotives ever built for a British railway also put in its appearance. Gresley collaborated with the engineers of the Beyer,

15

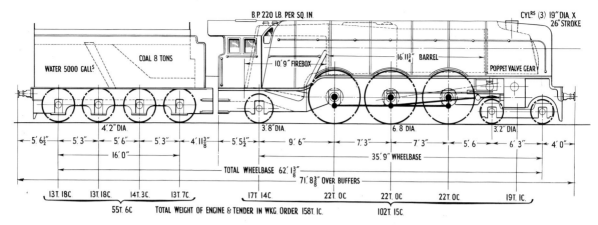

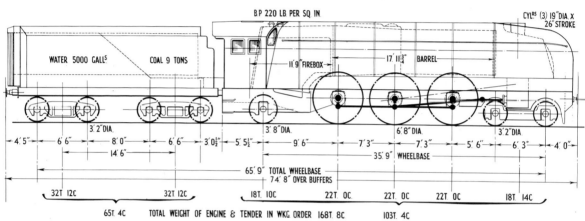

Above: Schemes prepared in May 1934 (top) and March 1935 (bottom), during development of the Class A4 Pacific; showing a transition from a layout similar to the Class P2 2-8-2 as built, towards a more fully streamlined outer casing.

Peacock & Co Ltd works at Gorton, near Manchester, to produce a huge Garratt type engine designed specially for banking duties at Wentworth, on the line between Wath marshalling yard and Penistone. With a tractive effort of 72,490lb this was a true giant—like two of Gresley's '02' freight 2-8-0s placed end to end. Only one was ever built because the specific need required no further examples. The two sets of three cylinders and motion were standard with an '02', but the boiler was a special design produced by Beyer, Peacock to Gresley's requirement.

A further stage in Gresley's application of the three-cylinder arrangement took place in the autumn of 1927, when the first Class D49 4-4-0 appeared (No 234 *Yorkshire*) of a type intended for intermediate express passenger duties. The three cylinders were arranged to drive on to the leading pair of coupled wheels and the boiler used was the same as that produced by Gresley for the 'J39' 0-6-0 goods engines.

The Pacifics had been much improved by the application of long-travel valves, but Gresley was still not satisfied and he next began to experiment with higher boiler pressures. He fitted one of the early 'A1's, No 4480 *Enterprise,* with a new boiler, with the higher working pressure of 220lb per sq in, at the same time enlarging the superheater. Further tests were carried out, with altered cylinder dimensions, on No 2544 *Lemburg* and in due course a design was prepared for what was known as the new 'Super Pacific', or Class A3, which is described in detail in Section 15.

With the creation of the 'A3' class the first phase of Gresley's career came to fulfilment. For the sake of pictorial continuity the subsequent careers of the various Gresley designs produced between 1911-1927 are dealt with, up to and including BR days, and the reader cannot fail to be impressed by both the longevity and the reliability of the various designs produced during the period covered by this volume. Indeed the vast majority were still giving faithful service some 30 years later. The real triumphs of the Gresley regime were still to come, culminating of course with the world record breaking run of the 'A4' Pacific *Mallard* in 1938.

It was in the period 1928-1941 that Gresley's work and personal career was to attain its greatest heights. Between those years he gave the London & North Eastern Railway a stud of steam locomotives par excellence. The name Gresley became synonymous with steam, speed and streamlining. The achievements both of the man and of his machines were the result of painstaking and critical attention to the fundamentals of steam locomotive design.

Gresley's forward-looking 'big engine' policy was in marked contrast to the contemporary activities of the neighbouring LMSR, where the influence of Derby still remained firm, and double-heading with medium-sized locomotives was a commonplace procedure. Indeed, in 1928 the Fowler 'Royal Scot' class 4-6-0s were only a year old, and these represented an urgent and belated attempt to enter the 'big engine' field by the LMSR.

The early years of the LNER witnessed progressive use of Gresley's favoured three-cylinder layout for new engines. By 1928 there had been added to those mentioned earlier a large number of Pacifics, including the improved 'Super Pacific', (the Class A3) and in that year the Pacific hauled non-stop 'Flying Scotsman' express between London and Edinburgh was inaugurated, on 1 May. Further examples of the Class D49 4-4-0, showed some variations in the valve gear used for the three cylinders, with some engines featuring poppet valves, some of them with a rotary cam gear to operate the valves. Clearly, Gresley was not content

to rest on his laurels where valve gear design was concerned, and was keeping an open mind on the subject.

A new three-cylinder 4-6-0 design, the Class B17 was introduced in 1928, specifically for the former Great Eastern routes. The 'B17s' were the only Gresley engines to have divided drive, with the two outside cylinders driving on the second coupled axle, and the inside cylinder driving on the leading coupled axle; an arrangement imposed by the civil engineer's weight limitations.

Behind the scenes in 1928 and in an atmosphere of some secrecy an experimental locomotive was being produced by Gresley, featuring a high-pressure boiler and a four-cylinder compound layout. This was the Class W1 4-6-4 which emerged from Darlington works in December 1929 and, because of the secrecy surrounding its development, soon gained the nickname of 'Hush-Hush'. In service the engine proved somewhat troublesome and did not come up to Gresley's expectations, in particular by burning considerably more coal than a Pacific. After eight years, during which considerable modifications were made, it was rebuilt as a three-cylinder simple, with streamlined outer casing.

Mention of streamlining brings me to one particular contribution Gresley made to British locomotive design; namely the dramatic change in the outer form of his largest engines. In the case of the Class W1 high-pressure design as first built, this change was largely dictated by the physical dimensions of the water tube boiler, which had to be

Left: The wedge-shaped front end finally adopted for the streamlined Class A4 Pacifics was inspired by the shape used by Ettore Bugatti for some French railcars, and was subsequently developed by Gresley using wind-tunnel tests upon wooden scale models, before the drawings were finalised. With its presentation bell ringing, No 4489 *Dominion of Canada* displays the sleek lines of the streamlined engine and carriages to perfection. The streamlining effectively saved horsepower and fuel consumption in the higher speed ranges. *LPC*

confined within the LNER loading gauge. The engine was not streamlined, but the attention paid to the airflows at the front end in order to lift the exhaust clear of the driving cab resulted in a novel-looking steam locomotive, and one which aroused considerable public interest.

This rejection of the classic British steam locomotive lineaments was to manifest itself a second time in the outer appearance of the Class P2 Mikados of 1934. But first we must mention another new design, the Class V1 2-6-2T three-cylinder tank engine design, introduced in 1930. This was to prove to be the only new three-cylinder tank engine design produced by Gresley for the LNER, although various schemes for other types were contemplated, including the 2-6-4T and the 2-8-2T wheel arrangement.

The aforementioned Class P2 Mikados were a specialised design, for the heavily graded Edinburgh-Aberdeen route, and were intended to haul the heavy passenger trains at higher average speeds. The 2-8-2 wheel arrangement was selected to obtain good adhesion, but this was to prove troublesome on some of the severe curves encountered on that route; resulting in high maintenance costs for the motion and bearings. The outer appearance of the first two engines featured a front end layout not dissimilar to the 'Hush-Hush' 4-6-4, and the shape of the smokebox top with stovepipe double chimney, and the wing plates, extended forward from the boiler casing, was the result of wind tunnel experiments undertaken by the City and Guilds (Engineering) College. A further modification to existing practice was the use of a wedge-shaped front to the cab. In France, the PLM railway had extensively used such a feature for many years; having found that it gave an improved lookout with reduced glare from the fire at night, and assisted in dispersing exhaust.

An interesting discovery was made, namely that whilst the first engine (which was fitted with rotary cam poppet valves) lifted the exhaust quite well, the second engine (which was fitted with the standard three-cylinder Walschaerts gear) did not clear the smoke from the driver's vision when being worked at early cut-offs. A second set of deflector plates had to be fitted to this engine specifically to overcome this problem.

In the outside world, the appearance of these two engines made quite an impression, and subsequently there were one or two instances of Continental locomotive engineers closely following Gresley's front end screening for new designs of their own; in particular by Cockerill of the Belgian National Railways, who closely copied it for his four-cylinder Pacifics (also, incidentally having to add a second set of deflectors!). In Britain, the later work of O.V.S. Bulleid for the Southern Railway – in the form of his air-smoothed Pacifics – also showed some derivation. Bulleid was Gresley's personal assistant when the Mikados were being designed, and it is thought that Bulleid had an important part to play in their final appearance. It was he who took the first engine, No 2001 *Cock o' the North* to France, for trials. (See page 114.)

French influence was in fact quite strong on LNER design development during the 1930s. Bulleid had worked in France as an engineer earlier in his career, and was fully conversant with the language, whilst Gresley himself took a close interest in the work of his French contemporary, André Chapelon on the Paris-Orleans Railway. Chapelon was obtaining excellent results from his rebuilt compound locomotives, and Gresley kept closely in touch with

Below: Bugatti's influence is readily apparent in this picture of the tail end observation car of the 1937 'Coronation' train. It could be argued that the reduced depth of the rear windows defeated the object of presenting a panoramic view, to some extent! Note the twin tail lamps carried, and the stainless steel lettering and numerals. *British Rail ER*

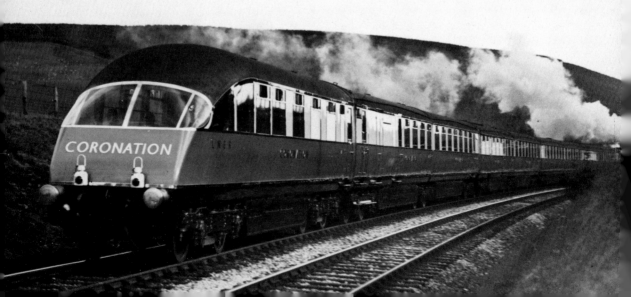

him. In particular, Chapelon had demonstrated the importance of enlarged and streamlined *inside* steam passages and ports, and had fitted the Kylchap double blastpipe and chimney, producing exceptionally free-steaming engines. He also employed the ACFI feedwater heater (which Gresley had fitted experimentally to some LNER engines). For the Mikados, Gresley used the knowledge he had gained from Chapelon, including the Kylchap exhaust and the ACFI feedwater heater, but he retained his three-cylinder layout as opposed to the four-cylinder compound arrangement favoured in France, and he decided upon the 2-8-2 layout with wide firebox, rather than the 4-8-0 layout that Chapelon favoured for routes of similar nature in France.

By the time Gresley's first Class P2 2-8-2, No 2001 *Cock o' the North* made its appearance, another factor was beginning to influence railway affairs, and one which was to have important effects upon Gresley's work for the LNER from 1934 onwards. This factor was the greatly increased competition now presented by alternative modes of transport; by road and by air. The railway companies had perforce carried the bulk of the burden of World War 1 transportation, and in the following years they had received far less than was due to them in terms of the government aid and support which was necessary in order to put them back on their feet. Meanwhile, the use of road vehicles (developed considerably during the war years), and the parallel development of the civil airliner, were both blossoming. Hence, by 1934, the LNER was faced with a commercial need to improve its major services to the public, both in order to maintain existing traffic, and to build a new enterprise which would establish a pattern for the future. Such alas, is the world of commerce.

With hindsight we can also see that another emergent factor was the use of oil, as opposed to coal, as the fuel for railway motive power. In Germany and North America considerable progress was being made with the use of the diesel engine as the prime mover for passenger trains. Allied to this was a desire for greater speed, one result of which was the scientific study of the applied art of streamlining, whereby the form of the front end of the locomotive, or train, was shaped in such a way as to reduce wind resistance. Theoretically this allowed greater speeds and reduced fuel consumption, although in some of the early cases in Germany and North America it is doubtful whether the added weight (and the increased fuel and maintenance costs) really justified the work involved.

Gresley's entry into the field of streamlining resulted from the interest shown by the LNER Directors in the exploits of a two-car articulated diesel-electric high speed train prototype, built in 1932 by the German firm of Wagen und Maschinenbau AG. This went into service between Berlin and Hamburg in May 1933, and was known as the 'Flying Hamburger'. It had a top speed of nearly 100mph. The LNER Directors were sufficiently impressed to ask Gresley to approach the German makers, to obtain costs and data for a three-coach articulated diesel set to run between London and Newcastle. This he did, but they could only promise a 4¼ hours minimum timing for the 268 miles, and the accommodation for only 140 passengers would be quite spartan, with catering limited to cold buffet meals. The LNER General Manager felt this to be an unacceptable reduction in passenger comfort, and he was of the opinion that the same high speed timing could be achieved by a steam locomotive, hauling a limited load of standard passenger carriages and offering better amenities.

To establish whether this was a feasible alternative, Gresley arranged for a trial run to be made, using his Pacific locomotive No 4472 *Flying Scotsman*, with his personal assistant, O.V.S. Bulleid, on the footplate as an observer. With four coaches, the engine ran the 185 miles from Kings Cross to Leeds in 151min 56sec; achieving a maximum speed of 95mph. With two more coaches added, the engine achieved a maximum of 100mph on the return run. A second test was held, between London and Newcastle, using Pacific No 2750 *Papyrus*, with seven coaches, in which a maximum of 108mph was reached. The tests showed that Gresley's steam Pacifics could hold their own against the German diesel set; it also showed a disadvantage of steam in that the driver and fireman had to work considerably harder. For the second test, Gresley had a fresh crew provided for the return run. Thus, the advent of the main line diesel was deferred for many years to come.

On a visit to France in 1933, Gresley had been deeply impressed by the reduction in wind resistance that had been achieved on some petrol-engined rail cars, designed by the racing car constructor Ettore Bugatti, which had a wedge-shaped end. This end seemed to allow the railcars to proceed at speed with very little head-resistance or tail slipstream. He realised that for a high speed steam locomotive, a similar streamlined form would be beneficial at the higher speed ranges. Accordingly, when the LNER Directors authorised the construction of a high speed steam-hauled train, early in 1935, Gresley was already interested in the problems of reducing wind resistance, and the streamlined form finally adopted for the new Pacifics, which were to haul the new train, resulted from serious scientific study, and not from any cheapjack publicity stunt. Using wooden models, tests were undertaken to evolve a satisfactory shape for the front end, the chimney and the outer cladding of the locomotive. These tests also demonstrated that by streamlining both the locomotive and the train itself, a reduction could be achieved in the horsepower needed to maintain

Right: Sir Nigel Gresley (left) on the footplate of Class A4 Pacific No 4489 *Dominion of Canada,* with Hon Vincent Massey in the cab, at the naming ceremony held at Kings Cross on 15 June 1937. Stainless steel polished Gill Sans numerals and coat-of-arms on plate attached to cabside.

high speeds against head-on wind resistance, with a consequent saving in fuel.

The streamlined Class A4 Pacific, which was the outcome of all this development work, was designed to haul the 'Silver Jubilee' train, which entered service between Newcastle and London in September 1935. This distance of 268 miles, with one stop en route at Darlington, was to be covered in four hours. The 232 miles from Darlington to London were booked to be worked at an average speed of 71mph, with some fast uphill running. So successful were the first of the streamlined Class A4 Pacifics once in service, that between 1935 and 1938 a total of 35 were built and they worked both the special limited load high speed trains and the considerably heavier normal main line trains, with equal mastery. During high speed brake trials on 3 July 1938, No 4468 *Mallard* (one of four engines built new with a double chimney), attained a world speed record of 126mph, whilst hauling a load of 236½ tons on a downhill section, and in so doing, placed the name of Gresley forever in the forefront of the 150 year saga of the British steam locomotive.

Although this present work is concerned with the locomotives of Nigel Gresley, it would be an injustice to the tremendous design effort of both Gresley and Bulleid, not to make at least brief mention here of the LNER streamlined trains as an ensemble. The first trains were finished in striking silver grey livery, and the interiors of the carriages were of improved, but simple appearance and comfort. The carriage exteriors were given a very smooth finish, with the spaces between the body ends sheeted over with indiarubber, and with steel valances below the bodysides between the bogies. In 1937 further streamlined trainsets were delivered, for the 'Coronation' and other services, and here the livery was changed to a rich garter blue for the Class A4 Pacifics, and a two-tone garter blue and

marlborough blue for the carriages. For the 'Coronation' train a special streamlined observation car was added, and this had a striking similarity to the wedge-shaped French Bugatti railcars, in the surface form of the tail end. The carriage interiors were both sumptuous and imaginative in their decor, for which Gresley called upon the services of his friend the interior designer Sir Charles Allom, of White Allom Ltd. The overall appearance of the trains, and the high speed services they provided, were a tremendous public relations asset to the LNER, and provoked considerable rivalry with the LMSR so far as the Anglo-Scottish services were concerned.

The magnificent Class A4 Pacifics could well be described as representing the pinnacle of Nigel Gresley's achievements. It is however worthwhile recalling that, had the Second World War not intervened, he had an improved 'A4' in preparation (with 275lb per sq in boiler pressure and tractive effort increased from 35,544lb to 39,040lb). He had also realised there was a need for an engine capable of working the heavy day-to-day express passenger trains at greater average speeds, by means of improved uphill running, and a scheme was prepared for a large 4-8-2 type, with a tractive effort of 45,700lb (see page 21). Other designs which came to nought included one for a three-cylinder articulated domeless 2-6-4-4 engine and tender type (to replace the Class K3 2-6-0s), but this was abandoned in favour of the three-cylinder Class V2 2-6-2 mixed traffic design; the first of which left Doncaster works in the summer of 1936. These 'V2s', or 'Green Arrows' were to prove most versatile and powerful locomotives and did some prodigious work during the grim war years. Another scheme which did not materialise, also reproduced on page 21, was for a 4-6-0 which was intended as an improvement upon both the 'K3' 2-6-0 and the 'B17'

4-6-0 types. This would have featured a large taper boiler and Pacific-type cylinders and front end arrangement.

The particularly arduous duties performed by the Class K2 2-6-0s allocated to the West Highland line, between Glasgow and Fort William and Mallaig had reached a stage where the loads required regular double-heading. Thus, a new locomotive was requested of Gresley, and this had to conform to the Civil Engineer's bridge loading limits for the line. The new design, which emerged from Doncaster in the early part of 1937, was a three-cylinder 2-6-0, and was classified 'K4'. At an early stage, a proposal for a three-cylinder 2-8-0 had been considered. The new Mogul had a 40 per cent increase in tractive effort, over the 'K2' class (later increased to 56 per cent when the boiler pressure was increased). The 'K4' boiler was a version of the boiler used on the Class B17 4-6-0s, and the new engines proved good steamers, capable of handling loads of up to 300 tons single handed, compared to the maximum of 220 tons for a Class K2 working solo.

The latter part of the 1930s saw the heyday of the big Gresley engines. The superb streamlined high speed trains were widely admired, and the 'big engine' fleet was kept in well-tuned shape, with the earlier Class A3s working happily alongside the 'A4s'. One area of locomotive policy remained to be attended to however; namely the use on secondary main line trains and the branch lines of ageing locomotives which had been supplanted on express duties by newer and larger types. They were a very mixed bag and it was realised that real economies

Below: Three Gresley 'might-have-beens'. A three-cylinder 4-8-2 for heavy express passenger trains; an improved 4-6-0 to replace the 'B17' and 'K3' classes, and a 2-6-4-4 articulated engine and tender design (which was abandoned in favour of the Class V2 2-6-2). *Photomatic*

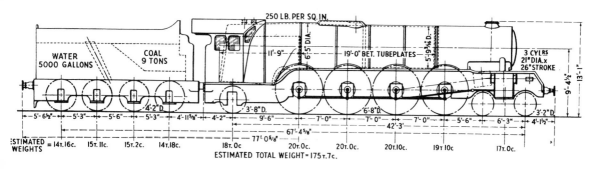

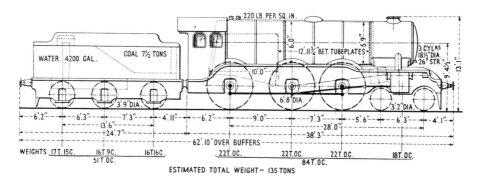

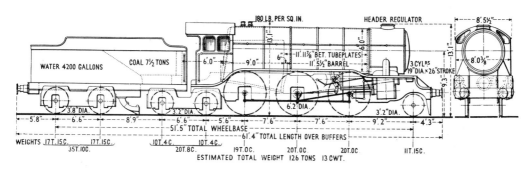

could be achieved if a new design of locomotive, of medium power and very wide route availability, could be designed to replace them. Gresley's solution was a three-cylinder 2-6-2 (a sort of scaled-down Class V2), of lightweight conception in order to suit the Civil Engineer's limitations for the types of route involved. The axle load of the Class V4, as it became known, was only 17 tons and the type was therefore suitable for use over some 5,000 route miles of the LNER. For comparison, it should be noted that the bigger Class V2 mixed-traffic 2-6-2 could only run over 2,752 miles.

Gresley's personal assistant O.V.S. Bulleid had left the LNER to become Chief Mechanical Engineer of the Southern Railway in May 1937, and these final 2-6-0 and 2-6-2 designs for the LNER probably had little or no Bulleid influence. Significantly, on the SR Bulleid was concurrently planning a 4-8-2 (just as Doncaster were also doing) which was to be for fast mixed-traffic use. Later this was changed to a 2-8-2 (shades of the 'P2' class) and it finally emerged as a Pacific – the famous 'Merchant Navy' class, which is described in a companion volume in this series.* In retrospect it seems that some of the most inventive features of the later Gresley years were influenced quite strongly by Bulleid, and one can only speculate what form any further Gresley designs might have taken, had Bulleid remained on the LNER.

Two factors must be taken into account when considering Gresley's last years in office. One was his own failing health, the other was the build up to and outbreak of World War 2. In fact Gresley was due to retire in June 1941, after some 29 years in office for the GNR and LNER. He died just two months earlier, from heart failure, at the age of 64.

In 1941 his engines were, in common with those of the other main line railways, probably being worked harder, and receiving less maintenance and attention than at any other time before or since in their careers. The depths of war, with abnormally heavy trainloads of men and materials, the hazards of enemy bombing, the strictures of the night-time blackout precautions, the shortage of young men (called-up to the armed forces), all these were adding to the normal daily problems which constitute the business of running a railway. Some of the more refined features of Gresley's engines, in particular his three-cylinder types, were showing signs of suffering from strain and neglect, and were coming under scrutiny because of a design philosophy rapidly gaining strength that future engines would have to be very simple and rugged in concept. This policy was, of course, to see the light of day on the LNER when Edward Thompson succeeded Gresley as CME (see Appendix 2). Perhaps, if he had lived to see it, Gresley – with his broad-minded outlook – would have come to terms with this changed attitude to locomotive design. But we shall never know.

What more heartening note on which to end this Introduction, however, than to recall the wonderful rejuvenation of some of his Pacifics, with double chimneys, which was to take place under BR auspices. The work done at Doncaster to improve the steaming of the 'A3s' and 'A4s' enabled both classes to perform outstandingly in their final years, still on main line duties and often deputising for a failed diesel locomotive. The standards of maintenance, and the quality of everyday running reflected the pride the footplate and shed men had in the Gresley engines in their final years on the East Coast Main Line. They have earned a great place in history.

As with the earlier titles in this series, I have selected the illustrations to emphasise the various detail alterations made to the various classes in the many stages of their careers. Each design is dealt with in chronological order, and the Appendices give details of various rebuilds, named locomotives, railcars and other relevant features of the Gresley régime. It is my earnest hope that the overall picture presented to the reader does proper justice to the immense contribution Sir Nigel Gresley made to the story of the British steam locomotive. Few men have been his equal in the saga of steam, anywhere in the world.

Once again, throughout the many hours of preparation which were required for this book, I have had the invaluable and generous assistance of many people. In particular I wish to thank my friend Alec Swain for some important initial groundwork, and A. B. MacLeod of the Ian Allan Library for his assistance in locating some elusive illustrations. Many people have heeded my requests for pictures and information, and in particular I would like to thank the following: H. C. Casserley; J. Edgington; L. Elsey; G. W. Goslin; T. G. Hepburn; K. Hoole; Messrs Photomatic Ltd; Peter Rowledge and Messrs Real Photographs Ltd. The line drawings include some specially drawn by Peter Winding for the author; other line drawings are reproduced by courtesy of *The Railway Gazette* and Ian Allan Library. My sincere thanks also to the National Railway Museum for the provision of some official LNER photographs.

One invaluable source of information must be acknowledged at this stage. I refer to the comprehensive and learned partwork which is still being produced by the Railway Correspondence & Travel Society, entitled *Locomotives of the LNER*. In this the Gresley designs are receiving all due attention and the reader in search of the most detailed information on all the classes of locomotive is strongly recommended to consult this fountain of knowledge. Other books of related interest are listed in the Bibliography.

Brian Haresnape, FRSA, NDD
Dorking, Surrey. November 1980

*Bulleid Locomotives, a Pictorial History by Brian Haresnape, Ian Allan Ltd.

Locomotives for the Great Northern Railway 1912 – 1922

SECTION 1

2-6-0 GNR Class H2, LNER Class K1
Mixed-Traffic Engines
Introduced: 1912
Total: 10

The locomotive students of 1912 must have awaited the appearance of the first of these Moguls with considerable interest, as it represented the first real indication of the new Gresley régime at work. The need was for a mixed-traffic locomotive and Gresley adopted the 2-6-0 wheel arrangement, with two outside cylinders of 20in diameter by 26in stroke and Walschaerts valve gear, and with the running plate raised high over the driving wheels. Many design features followed the Doncaster traditions as established under Stirling and Ivatt, in particular the cab, footplate fittings and tender, but the new engine was sufficiently different in appearance to have a 'modern' air about it.

The boiler was a rather modest affair, with a pressure of 170lb per sq in and with a diameter of only 4ft 8in, and this allowed room for a tall chimney and dome within the GNR loading gauge, perhaps making the design appear rather less powerful than it actually proved to be. The pony truck on the first engine had 3ft 8in diameter wheels, but the following nine engines had this reduced to 3ft 2in; with slight alteration to the front end frame design. Gresley used his own patent double-bolster swing-link type pony truck, but the engines were noted to be somewhat lively riders and this feature led to them (and later 2-6-0s) gaining the nickname of 'the Ragtimers', after a dance craze of the period.

Rough-riding apart, the class established themselves as hard working engines. To begin with, the first five were allocated to Kings Cross and worked fast goods turns to Peterborough and back, as well as some longer runs to Doncaster. Later they were to be found at Peterborough and Doncaster sheds and by then they were also used on secondary passenger and excursion train duties. Their livery when new was GNR apple green passenger colour with dark olive green edging. During World War 1, when these 10 Moguls did much valuable hard work on troop trains and heavy goods, they were repainted in the economy grey livery. The LNER painted them in its black, lined with red, mixed-traffic livery.

The engines were built as follows:

| No 1630 | Doncaster | 1912 |
| Nos 1631-1639 | Doncaster | 1913 |

Gresley decided to rebuild the class with larger boilers, making them in effect Class H3, LNER Class K2, (see Section 4), and this took place between June 1920 and July 1937, when the small-boilered class thus became extinct.

None preserved

The basic dimensions of the class were as follows:

Heating surface, tubes
  Large and small: 981sq ft
  Firebox: 137sq ft
Total (evaporative): 1,118sq ft
Superheater: 303sq ft
  Combined heating surfaces: 1,421sq ft
  Superheater elements: 18
Grate area: 12.6sq ft
Tractive effort (at 85 per cent BP): 22,070lb

Below: The diagram depicts the first engine of the class, with 3ft 8in diameter pony truck wheels. The following nine engines had this reduced to 3ft 2in.

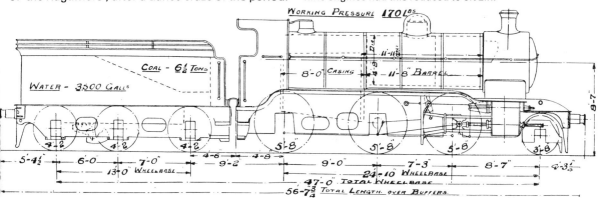

Above: Class H2 (LNER K1) two-cylinder Mogul No 1634, in original condition and painted in the full GNR passenger colours of apple green, despite the fact that Gresley envisaged them as mixed-traffic engines. Piston tail rods were originally fitted. The tender design was the existing GNR class B type, with a capacity of 3,500gal of water and 6½ton of coal, although as can be seen in this illustration the tender could be heaped to carry extra. *Ian Allan Library*

Right: The small-boilered Moguls found their way on to suburban passenger and excursion train workings, and No 1631 is seen here going along in fine style on a train which is headed by three six-wheeled carriages, followed by some heavy bogie stock. These larger and heavier bogie carriages were the basic reason for Gresley's move towards larger-boilered and bigger locomotive designs – his so-called 'big engine' policy. *H. Gordon Tidey*

Bottom right: Class K1 small-boiler 2-6-0 No 4638 in LNER days, still in its original condition apart from the fitting of outside steampipes to the cylinders, and the removal of the piston tail rods. The LNER livery was black with red lining, although the red lining was not always visible to the camera, due to the type of film available. Note the LNER renumbering to No 4638, the class becoming Nos 4630-4639 (although Nos 4631/35 had by then been rebuilt to Class K2). Some of these engines received smaller chimneys in LNER days. *Photomatic*

SECTION 2

2-8-0 GNR Class 01, LNER Class 01, 03 after 1944, BR Power Class 8F
Heavy Goods Engines
Introduced: 1913
Total: 20

When a larger heavy goods engine than the excellent but hard-pressed Ivatt 'Long Tom' 0-8-0s became an urgent necessity, for the Peterborough-London coal traffic in particular, Gresley again utilised a pony truck to provide the greater length required for a bigger boiler, and for two outside cylinders with Walschaerts valve gear. The cylinders were of 21in by 28in and drove on to coupled wheels of 4ft 8in diameter. The new boiler, the largest produced by Doncaster to that date, was a logical development of the Ivatt design. In most respects the design of the 2-8-0 echoed the features of Gresley's pioneer Moguls, and the same mixture of modern and traditional design features was apparent. The cab and tender followed Great Northern traditions, except that the front spectacle plate was enlarged in size, whereas the front end featured the modern layout created for the Moguls. A feature of these engines was the use of a Robinson superheater with a high degree of superheat (see table below).

Like their Churchward counterparts on the GWR, these basically strong and simple goods engines proved to be well suited to their tasks. The nickname of 'Tangos' was bestowed upon them by the enginemen, because their valve motion made a noticeable clanking sound when in movement.

The engines were built as follows:

Nos 456-460   Doncaster   1913/14
Nos 462-476   North British   1919/20

The construction of Nos 462-476, by the North British Locomotive Company, is an interesting reflection upon the chaos created by war. Basically the order for the first 10 came about because the GNR was short of eight-coupled freight engines, having lent 10 'Long Toms' to the North Eastern Railway, which had earlier sent the same number of its own engines of similar type to France. Gresley proposed construction of 10 more 'Tangos' to replace the lost motive power. The current steel shortage was such that Gresley ordered the bulk of material required – for frames, axles, tyres boiler plates, etc – from America. By the time this material arrived in Britain, the situation at Doncaster was such that they could not build the engines and Gresley asked the North British Locomotive Company to undertake the construction, using the American materials. The order was increased to 15, with the first 10 erected at NBL's Hyde Park works in Glasgow and the last five in its Atlas works, also in Glasgow.

The LNER twice renumbered the engines; at first they became Nos 3456-3460, 3462-3476 respectively, and then (in 1946) Nos 3475-3479, 3480-3494 respectively. In BR days 60000 was added to these numbers.

Last of class withdrawn: No 63484 (1952)
None preserved

The basic dimensions of the class were as follows:

Heating surface, tubes
  Large and small: 1,922sq ft
  Firebox: 162sq ft
Total (evaporative): 2,084sq ft
Superheater: 570sq ft
  Combined heating surfaces: 2,654sq ft
  Superheater elements: 24
Grate area: 27sq ft
Tractive effort (at 85 per cent BP): 31,860lb

Below: Gresley's Class 01 2-8-0 of 1913, with a modern front end and valve gear married to traditional GNR features. Note the unequal spacing of the tender wheelbase.

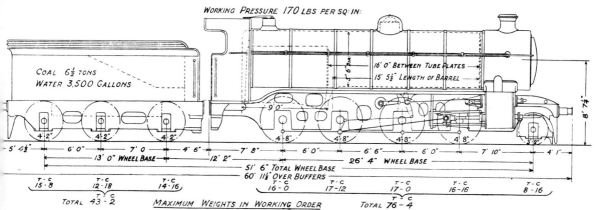

Left: No 473 of the final North British Locomotive Company batch, finished in grey livery with some lining out on boiler bands and footplating, but not on the tender. Long piston tailrods fitted to cylinders. *Photomatic*

Below left: Working hard through New Southgate with a mixed freight, No 460 has five cattle wagons next to the tender (whitewashed as a precaution to protect livestock during Summer heat). These two-cylinder simple 2-8-0s quickly proved their worth, but Gresley had even better ideas for heavy freight engines germinating in his mind, even whilst these 'Tangos' were being built. *H. Gordon Tidey*

Above: Class O1 two-cylinder 2-8-0 No 476, fitted with an experimental feedwater device. *LPC*

Left: LNER No 3456, originally GNR No 456, the first of the class. Still in basically original condition, complete with piston tail rods. Livery in LNER days was originally black with red lining out. These two-cylinder 2-8-0s were never in the limelight, compared to his later three-cylinder engines, and all were withdrawn by BR by 1953. *LPC*

Bottom left: Class O1 2-8-0 No 3466, with front end indicator shelter fitted, and attached to the former NER dynamometer car, seen working extremely hard on a test train of coal wagons between Peterborough and Ferme Park yard in February 1925. The object was to compare the performance of the two-cylinder 2-8-0 with three-cylinder Class O2 No 3479. The latter showed an economy in coal and water consumption. *Ian Allan Library*

0-6-0T GNR Class J23, LNER Class J50/J51*, BR Power Class 4F
Shunting Tank Engines
Introduced: 1913* 1922
Total: (30*) 102

The 0-6-0 saddle tank was favoured for shunting and local trip work by the GNR until the appearance of Gresley's first tank engine design, which was an 0-6-0T with long side tanks. These side tanks were tapered at the front, to allow the driver adequate forward vision, and had an aperture providing access to the inside valve motion. The change to side tanks of this pattern was partly because the first batch of engines was intended for use in the West Riding area, where the steep gradients made maximum adhesive weight desirable, although it transpired that the first examples built had an unsatisfactory weight distribution, which was solved in the interim by blanking-off part of the side tank water capacity at the front end, and adding it to the bunker.

The new engines were designed to take secondhand boilers from Ivatt 0-8-2Ts, which were currently receiving new and larger boilers. This availability of some 40 surplus, but sound, boilers of 4ft 2in diameter meant that Gresley could produce a batch of new engines at comparatively low cost, although the boiler barrels had to be shortened to suit a six-coupled wheelbase. Three of the boilers used were in fact originally intended for Stirling single-wheelers (only one was actually fitted, to No

*The 30 original 'J23' (LNER 'J51') were all rebuilt to Class J50 between 1929 and 1935.

Below: The drawing depicts the later version, Class J50, first introduced in 1922 as the 221 series Class J23, with larger 4ft 5in diameter boiler and larger coal bunker.

872 in 1900) and had subsequently been used on 0-8-2Ts. The first batch of 10 locomotives included one, No 167, built at Doncaster in 1914 which was superheated as an experiment, which if successful would have been applied to the whole class. The Robinson superheater had to be adapted to suit the boiler size and with 16 elements was somewhat smaller than normal in contemporary Doncaster practice.

Another feature tried out on No 167 was a mechanical lubricator, feeding oil to the cylinders which were experimentally equipped with balanced slide valves in place of the usual flat valves. These features of No 167 did not prove of any significant advantage to the engine on the sort of duties the class performed, and indeed the engine even gained a reputation for being sluggish compared to the saturated steam version, and no further examples of the class received superheating, or balanced slide valves.

The coal bunker capacity of the first 10 locomotives, reduced by the auxiliary water tank, was increased by adding coal rails to form a cage between the rear cab windows, up to roof level, after it was found the original provision was inadequate. This increase was from 2 tons approximately, to 3 tons 4cwt. Later batches of engines had increased bunker capacity without a water tank and on longer frames, making the coal cage unnecessary.

A total of 30 engines were built with the 4ft 2in boilers, between 1913-19 and the principal dimensions of these, as delivered, were as follows: two inside cylinders 18in diameter by 26in stroke driving on to coupled wheels of 4ft 8in diameter; the boiler (except No 167 with superheater) had a working pressure of 175lb; heating surface comprised: tubes, 869sq ft; firebox, 111sq ft; making a total of 980sq ft. On No 167, the cylinders were increased to 18½in diameter and the boiler pressure was 170lb. The heating surface, with superheater added, comprised: tubes, 605sq ft; firebox, 111sq ft; and superheater, 229sq ft; making a total of 945sq ft. The grate area on all 30 locomotives was 17¾sq ft. Exact weight varied, but typically was about 56 tons in

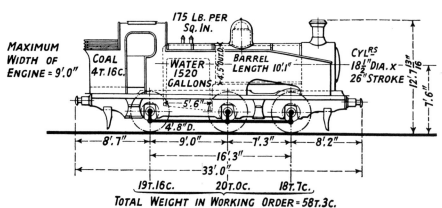

Above: The solitary superheated engine, No 167, delivered early in 1914, showing the mechanical lubricator carried on the running plate just behind the leading splasher, and the snifting valve behind the chimney. Finished in Gresley's slate grey livery, No 167 also shows the original provision of filler holes at the front end of the side tanks, for the front sandboxes, and the coal cage added to the small bunker of the initial 10 engines, known as the 157 series of GNR Class J23. *LPC*

Left: The second batch built, known as the 168 series, had an enlarged bunker, upon lengthened frames, and only one, No 173 seen here, carried a coal cage as well, for a period. The weight distribution was altered and the tanks once again held the full provision of water, without an auxiliary tank in the bunker. The footstep behind the leading coupled wheels was reduced in width, and the whistle resited lower on the cab front. *Ian Allan Library*

Bottom left: The 221 series was the last to be built to GNR design, some being delivered in 1922 and the rest in 1924, after the Grouping. These were designed to take larger 4ft 5in diameter secondhand boilers, and Nos 222-30 had a wider tapered chimney fitted. Although the GNR classified them as 'J23s', along with the earlier engines, the LNER made them Class J50 instead of 'J51'. *Photomatic*

Right: Class J50/2 No 3216, photographed at Ardsley on 27 June 1937. This engine was originally built in 1919 as GNR Class J23, 168 series, which became LNER Class J51, and was rebuilt to Class J50/2 in 1929. Coal rails, with solid backing plate added to bunker and front sandbox relocated to feed the centre coupled wheels, placed behind footstep. *H. C. Casserley*

Below: Two accident-damaged Gresley 'quad-art' suburban sets (with the ends stoved-in) are seen being worked as empty stock by 'J50/2' No 68931 past Oakleigh Park; 28 February 1953. *B. E. Morrison*

working order, with 1,500 gallons of water and 3 tons of coal. Tractive effort at 85% was 23,636lb.

Allowing for spares, the 30 engines just described accounted for the 4ft 2in boilers from the Ivatt 0-8-2Ts and Gresley next allocated surplus boilers of 4ft 5in diameter, from various tender engines which were either being withdrawn or reboilered. Some of these boilers were even older than the 4ft 2in version, and they soon had the pressure reduced from 175lb to 170lb, to give them a longer working life. The cylinder diameter was increased to 18½in and a larger coal bunker was fitted, carrying over 4 tons of coal, with the total weight in working order lighter, at 58 tons. In GNR days the larger-boilered engines were included in Class J23, but at the Grouping they became LNER Class J50 whereas the first 30 engines became Class J51. Basic dimensions are shown in the table below.

The 'J50' version was selected by the LNER for further construction, to 'Group Standard' specification, and the first examples began to emerge from Doncaster in March 1926. Detail changes included balanced wheels and larger axle journals, large

ventilator on the cab roof and under-footplate injectors. The new boilers supplied had Ross pop safety valves, in place of the original Ramsbottom type inside a casing. By 1929 the original 30 Class J51s, with the smaller boilers, were in need of reboilering, and between then and 1935 they received 4ft 5in boilers and were reclassified 'J50' (see list below).

The GNR engines were built as follows:

157 Series (LNER Class J51/1)

Nos 157-164/6/7	Doncaster	1913/4

168 Series (LNER Class J51/2)

Nos 168-176/8	Doncaster	1914/5
Nos 211-220	Doncaster	1919

Below: A classic view of a Class J50/2 performing the sort of task for which the design was originally conceived in GNR days. No 68925 heads a freight at Holbeck, in fine style. The first 30 GNR locomotives gained the nickname of 'Ardsley Tanks' because of their employment in the West Riding. *Eric Treacy*

Right: The 'J50/4' version was introduced in 1938 and featured a hopper type bunker and welded side tanks. Provision was made for steam heating to allow the engines to work empty carriage duties in winter months. No 68983 is seen leaving Copenhagen Tunnel with empty stock on 30 April 1955. In 1952 the 'J50/4', or 599 series, was incorporated in 'J50/3'. Note the lowered cab roof and raised ventilator of LNER Group Standard engines, also the raised tank fillers. Seven locomotives were transferred to Departmental stock and renumbered in the Department series by BR, starting with two withdrawn locos, Nos 68911/4, which became Nos 10 and 11 respectively for use at Doncaster Works, in 1961. The following year, Nos 68917/28/61/71/6 became Nos 12-16; also going to Doncaster for use in both the Locomotive and the Carriage & Wagon Works areas. All seven were replaced by diesel shunters in 1965. *B. E. Morrison*

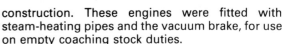

221 Series (LNER Class J50/2)

Nos 221-230	Doncaster	1922
Nos 3231-3240*	Doncaster	1924

The 30 engines of the 157 and 168 Series were rebuilt to conform to LNER Class J50 as follows:

1929: Nos 3157/9/66/76, 3211/4/6/7/20.
1930: Nos 3167/9/72/3, 3212/3/9.
1931: Nos 3160/70, 3215.
1932: Nos 3161/2/4/8/71/4/5, 3218.
1934: Nos 3163/78.
1935: No 3158.

The LNER 'Group Standard' engines, Class J50, were built as follows:

583 Series (LNER Class J50/3)

Nos 583/6/8/9/91/3/4/6, 601/3.	Doncaster	1926
Nos 609/10/6/7/8/21/2/35/6	Doncaster	1926
Nos 1037/41/5/58/63/8/9/70/4/9	Doncaster	1926/7
Nos 1081/2/6	Doncaster	1927
Nos 2789-2794	Doncaster	1930

599 Series (LNER Class J50/4)

Nos 599, 600/2/5/6/8/11/15	Gorton	1938/9
Nos 584/5/7/90/5/8	Gorton	1939

The 599 series, built at Gorton, had a modified bunker design, with a hopper top in place of coal rails and the side tanks were of all-welded construction. These engines were fitted with steam-heating pipes and the vacuum brake, for use on empty coaching stock duties.

As can be seen from the lists above, the numbers allocated to the engines when new were a random selection taken from blank numbers in the stock book. Not until Thompson's renumbering scheme of 1943 were all the engines of the type grouped together, becoming Nos 8890-8991, in order of construction. In 1948 British Railways added 60000 to these numbers as part of the Eastern Region block renumbering.

These strong tank engines were included in Thompson's postwar standardisation scheme, but no further examples were built because the LNER purchased 75 of the war surplus Ministry of Supply 0-6-0STs, of Hunslet design (becoming their Class J94) and these sufficed, together with the existing stock of 'J50s', until the advent of the diesel-electric shunters in BR days.

Last of class withdrawn: Nos 68911/4/7/28/61/71/6 (1965)*
None preserved

The basic dimensions for the Class J50 version were as follows:

Heating surface
  Tubes: 1,016sq ft
  Firebox: 103sq ft
Total: 1,119sq ft
No superheater
Grate area: 16.25sq ft
Tractive effort (at 85 per cent BP): 23,636lb

*LNER numbering 3000 was also added to the earlier locomotives listed, thus No 167 became No 3167 etc.

*These seven engines ran in Departmental stock, as Nos 10-16 prior to final withdrawal.

SECTION 4

2-6-0 GNR Class H3, LNER Class K2, BR Power Class 4MT
Mixed-Traffic Engines
Introduced: 1913
Total: 75*

Experience in service with the first 10 Moguls evidently led Gresley to decide to advance the design by providing a bigger boiler, of 5ft 6in diameter and 170lb per sq in pressure, fitted with a 24-element Robinson superheater. Basically the design was otherwise unchanged, with the same cylinders, valves, grate, wheels etc. The wheelbase was lengthened slightly, and the new engines weighed some 2 tons more. These engines, which later became known as the 'K2' class, quickly proved their worth and construction was pushed ahead early in 1914, to provide valuable mixed-traffic power for the GNR main line.

The engines were built as follows:

Nos 1640-1649	Doncaster	1913/14
Nos 1650-1659	Doncaster	1916
Nos 1660-1679	North British	1918
Nos 1680-1704	Kitson & Co	1920/21

(Of the North British engines, Nos 1660-1669 were built at the NBL Hyde Park works and Nos 1670-1679 were built at Queens Park.)

The fitting of outside steam pipes was standard from No 1660 onwards, and earlier engines were altered when due for repairs or overhaul.

Those engines in service during World War 1 were heavily utilised for the increased loads that were a feature of the period, even finding themselves on express passenger duties, for which they were not really designed. Their strength lay in their versatility. The first 10 engines were delivered in full

*Includes 10 engines rebuilt Class K1.

GNR passenger green livery, but the wartime batch from North British were delivered in the grey livery with white lettering. Some of the later Kitson engines received the GNR passenger green. In LNER days they carried the black lined red mixed-traffic livery, but after World War 2 some received apple green again, and one retained this colour until 1954, by which time BR was painting the class in the LNWR-style mixed-traffic black with lining of red, cream and grey.

The 10 original small-boilered Moguls were rebuilt with the larger boilers, becoming LNER Nos 4630-4639, and then Nos 1720-1729. Rebuilding took place over a period of 17 years commencing in 1920.

So useful did the 'K2' design prove to be that Gresley was asked to consider extending their route availability. This was necessary because the somewhat generous GNR loading gauge, to which they were designed, did not exist on certain other parts of the LNER system, in particular in Scotland and on the lines of the former Great Eastern Railway. This increase in route availability was achieved by the use of shorter chimneys and domes and the resiting of the whistle on the firebox top instead of on the cab roof.

When it was decided to transfer 14 of the class to Scotland for use on the West Highland line in 1925 (to be followed by a further six in 1931/2), some more noticeable modifications were made to their appearance, in particular the fitting of new low roof side-window cabs, following complaints of lack of comfort by the enginemen. These engines had deeper ashpans to suit the Scottish coal. Names of

Below: The drawing depicts the original GNR version of the class.

Scottish lochs were carried by the 13 engines regularly used on the West Highland line. The engines sent to the Great Eastern Section, also cut down in height, were fitted with the Westinghouse air brake. Another modification, of a temporary nature, was the fitting of Scarab oil-burning equipment to Nos 1641/67/8/9/71/4 during the 1921 coal strike.

The class were widespread in their allocation in later years, and the Scottish ones in particular reigned supreme on the West Highland until usurped by the transfer of some Stanier 'Black Five' 4-6-0s in BR days.

Last of class withdrawn: 61756 (1962)
None preserved

The basic dimensions of the class (as standardised by the LNER) were as follows:

Heating surface
  Tubes: 1,477sq ft
  Firebox: 152sq ft
Total: 1,629sq ft
Superheater: 305sq ft
Total Combined heating surfaces: 1,934sq ft
Grate area: 24.5sq ft
Tractive effort (at 85 per cent BP): 23,400lb

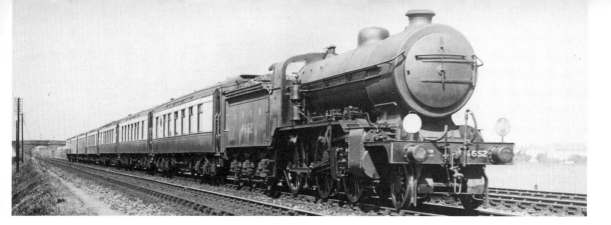

Left: The Kitson-built engines of 1920-21, Nos 1680-1704, were delivered with outside steampipes to the cylinders and two Ross 'pop' safety valves; features which eventually became standard for the entire class. No 1683 positively sparkles in this picture, finished in the apple green GNR livery scheme. Note the height of the chimney and the location of the whistle on the cab roof, features of the GNR engines when delivered. *H. Gordon Tidey*

Above: The down Sunday 'Clacton Pullman' seen passing Crowlands signalbox (between Chadwell Health and Romford), with Class K2 Mogul No 4652 at the head of the train. The engine is fitted with the Westinghouse air brake for working on the Great Eastern Section of the LNER, and also carries the disc headcodes that were a characteristic of the Section in steam days. Boiler mountings have been reduced in height to suit the GER loading gauge. *F. R. Hebron*

Below left: No 1655, of the 1916 Doncaster-built batch, finished in passenger green livery, and seen here in original condition, with piston tail rods fitted. These GNR engines had four Ramsbottom safety valves housed in the traditional style casing. *W. J. Reynolds*

Below: Still retaining the GNR tall chimney and dome, No 4661 was photographed at Doncaster in 1927, painted in the black lined red LNER mixed traffic livery, with number on the tender. *Photomatic*

Top right: The 'K2s' sent to Scotland had their boiler mountings reduced in height and in due course they received new side-window cabs. No 4701, however, is seen here before receiving the new cab, at Fort William in June 1934. The engine is in the black lined red livery, with numerals on cabside and small lettering on the tender. The 13 engines on the West Highland line received names. No 4701 was *Loch Laggan. Photomatic*

Centre right: The earliest days of nationalisation still saw some ex-LNER locomotives being repainted in the postwar apple green livery, as shown here on No 61783 *Loch Sheil,* photographed at Mallaig on 28 September 1948. Only the number and the tender insignia have been changed to the new identity. This view clearly shows the revised cab design produced for the West Highland line engines, with side window and glass deflector screens, and with the whistle resited on top of the firebox. *C. C. B. Herbert*

Below: Remarkably little changed over its years in service is this Great Eastern line 'K2', No 61777, with Westinghouse air brake still fitted. The engine is seen at the summit of Stanway bank, near Colchester on a Sunday excursion to Clacton in May 1951. *P. M. Alexander*

Above: With an ugly square-topped cover, presumably produced by Cowlairs to replace a damaged one, No 61792 is seen on the morning Speyside goods train, leaving Boat of Garten in September 1957. At the time of the photograph this engine was allocated to Keith shed. *W. J. V. Anderson*

Left: A snowplough attachment below the bufferbeam gives No 61788 a decidedly rakish air as it double-heads a Stanier 'Black Five'. The Stanier engines displaced the 'K2s' on the West Highland line after the Gresley engines had provided the power for this difficult route for more than a quarter of a century. *D. M. C. Hepburne-Scott*

SECTION 5

2-8-0 (3-cyl) GNR Class 461, LNER Class 02
Heavy Goods Engine
Introduced: 1918
Total: 1

Most people, if asked to name Gresley's most outstanding advance in locomotive design, would no doubt immediately select either his 'A3' Pacific *Flying Scotsman* or the record-breaking 'A4' *Mallard;* for such is the price of fame. However, the serious student of the steam locomotive may well, and justifiably, arrive at a very different answer. That answer would be the solitary initial Gresley three-cylinder locomotive, the 2-8-0 No 461 of 1918.

We have seen in the Introduction how Gresley examined the merits of multi-cylindered engines during the course of World War 1. It was, however, the simple two-cylinder layout that he applied to his new locomotives built during that period. His interest in multi-cylindered engines required both time for experiment and a better political climate before any actual construction could take place. As O.S. Nock has observed in his book, *The Locomotives of Sir Nigel Gresley,* the suitability of three-cylinder propulsion for heavy freight working had already been demonstrated convincingly by Wilson Worsdell, whose North Eastern Railway Class X 4-8-0Ts were successfully operating the Erimus hump yard. Gresley's own new two-cylinder 2-8-0s were doing an excellent job on the Peterborough-London coal trains, but the idea of a three-cylinder version, providing a more even crank effort and a smoother start away from rest, evidently held an appeal for him.

It was therefore a logical, but enterprising, step to take the boiler of his two-cylinder 2-8-0 design and supply its steam to three cylinders instead of two. These three cylinders, 18in by 26in, were arranged in line and drove on to the second pair of coupled wheels. To make this possible the cylinders had to

be steeply inclined, and the connecting rods were shorter than those of the two-cylinder engines. Where Gresley began to show his true colours was in the layout of the valve gear. He had devised a method of eliminating one of the three sets of gear, at first, on this engine, a rather complicated layout but one which he was soon to refine. No 461 must be regarded as a 'guinea-pig' and whilst trials were undertaken Gresley continued to have more of his two-cylinder 2-8-0s produced. Working on the Peterborough-London coal trains, the solitary three-cylinder engine soon demonstrated its superiority over the two-cylinder version, especially when starting a heavy load. In Gresley's mind the seal must have been set for future developments.

Visually, No 461 was a graceful machine with flowing curves to the footplating over the steeply inclined cylinders and with all the various Doncaster hallmarks, of cab, tender and chimney design.

The engine was built at Doncaster in 1918, and was withdrawn from service (as No 3921) in 1948.

The basic dimensions were as follows:

Heating surfaces, tubes
    Large and small: 1,868.5sq ft
    Firebox: 163.5sq ft
Total (evaporative): 2,032sq ft
Superheater: 430.5sq ft
    Combined heating surfaces: 2462.5sq ft
Grate area: 27.5sq ft
Tractive effort (at 85 per cent BP): 34,523lb

Below: Gresley's first three-cylinder 2-8-0, No 461 of 1918.

Right: Front end view of No 461 when new, showing layout of the inside cylinder and characteristically clean Doncaster finish to the detail design. *NRM*

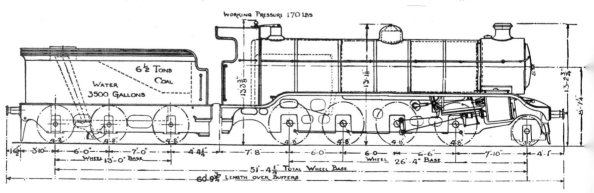

Right: In sparkling external condition, No 461 receives some attention from its crew during the course of a goods train working on the GNR main line. Trials with this engine, and a meeting with H. Holcroft of the SECR led to Gresley producing an improved three-cylinder 2-8-0 design, with conjugated valve gear, in 1921 (see Section 7). *Ian Allan Library*

Below: At New England shed in March 1935, and in LNER black livery, No 3461 (as it became after Grouping) shows surprisingly little detail change except for the substitution of two Ross 'pop' safety valves in place of the four Ramsbottom valves, and for the elongated dome casing, which housed an experimental top feed water-purifying apparatus, which Gresley tried out on several different engine types. *Photomatic*

SECTION 6

**2-6-0 (3-cyl) GNR Class H4, LNER Class K3,
BR Power Class 6MT
Mixed-Traffic Engines
Introduced**: 1920
Total: 193

If Gresley had commenced his locomotive designing career by producing a Mogul that was
somewhat underboilered, then by 1920 he must
have established a firm conviction that any new
engine would require a boiler of proportions ample
enough to meet all expected requirements without
being stretched to the limits. For in that year
Doncaster unveiled No 1000, the first 'H4' class
three-cylinder Mogul, with a boiler of 6ft diameter;
the first British engine to carry a boiler of that
diameter. This feature alone gave his new design a
most imposing and powerful appearance. The seal
was set for the Gresley 'style', although as yet he
was still apparently content to utilise the traditional
Doncaster style for the tender and cab.

The length of the new boiler was the same as that
on the 'H3' class, but the increased diameter gave it
a higher pitch and consequently a smaller chimney
and dome. Observers of the day were deeply
impressed by the 'modern' appearance of the front
end of the new design.

Perhaps the most important advance the 'H4'
demonstrated was, however, not the ample boiler,
but the layout and design of the valve gear. I have
already recounted, in the Introduction, how Gresley
obtained some expertise from H. Holcroft of the
SECR, on the subject of a conjugate arrangement for
three-cylinder engines. The design of valve gear
applied to the 'H4s', and to the later Pacifics and
numerous other types, was Gresley's solution.
There was also a new three-bar slidebar and small

crosshead, and very refined alloy steel rods for the
motion.

The Gresley conjugate arrangement had two sets
of Walschaerts gear to the outside cylinder. The
inside cylinder had the valve placed alongside the
cylinder instead of above, and this was actuated by
two horizontal rocking levers which were connected
to the tailrods at the front of the outside valve
chests. These levers were of unequal length, which
gave rise to the description of '2 to 1 motion'. The
cylinders were 18½in by 26in and had 8in piston
valves with 1½in lap.

Initially No 1000 and the following engines of the
batch were employed on fast goods trains, where
they soon earned themselves the nickname of
'Jazzers' (another allusion to a popular dance craze)
because, like Gresley's earlier Moguls, they proved
to be lively riders at speed. It was the 1921 coal strike
that was really to demonstrate the capabilities of the
new engines, however. Then they were put to work
on passenger trains, between Doncaster and
London. These trains were often combined to make
up one train of up to 19 coaches; some 600 tons or
more gross. On these terrific loads, 16 trips were
recorded where they kept to the scheduled average
of approximately 50mph, and burned a mean total
of only 51lb of coal per mile. It was evident to all
concerned that Gresley had produced a truly
exceptional design.

No more were built in GNR days, but after the
Grouping, when Gresley had been appointed CME
for the LNER, building was resumed for more
general use on the system. The first batch, known as
the 'K3' class, was constructed at Darlington in 1924,
and some modifications were made to reduce the
overall clearances, in particular by fitting a smaller
chimney and dome. The GNR pattern of cab and

Below: The drawing depicts the class as built and running
after the Grouping, to LNER standards. (Class K3/4 of
1930).

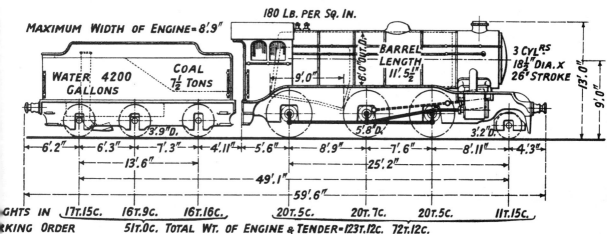

41

tender were replaced by a new side-window cab of decidedly NER appearance, and a new 'Group Standard' tender was attached. The design of the engine thus became a new LNER standard, and 183 were delivered between 1924 and 1937.

Changes were made to the cab design (raising the windows to more conventional height), and to the controls – placing the driver on the left of the footplate; this latter feature commencing with No 204 built at Darlington in 1924. Some older engines received this modification. A later version of the 'Group Standard' tender was also used; this had flush sides and gave the engine attached an even more up-to-date look. The numbering at first

Below: The famous pioneer three-cylinder Mogul, No 1000, in original condition, at the head of a fast GNR goods. Visually this engine established the Gresley style so far as the front end, boiler and wheels, motion and footplating were concerned but it still retained the traditional Doncaster cab and tender. No 1000 was finished in full apple green and olive green passenger livery. The chimney made full use of the generous GNR loading gauge. *Ian Allan Library*

applied was extremely haphazard, and simply utilised vacant numbers in the LNER list.

The engines were built as follows:

Nos (GNR) 1000-1009 (These became LNER Nos 4000-4009)	Doncaster	1920/21
Nos (LNER) 17/28/32/33/36/ 38/39/46	Darlington	1924
Nos 52/53/58/69/73/75/ 80/91/92/109	Darlington	1924
Nos 111/112/113/114/116/118/ 120/121/125	Darlington	1924
Nos 126/127/134/135/140/ 141/143/146/153/156/158/ 159/163/167/170/178/180	Darlington	1925
Nos 184/186/188/191/195 200/203/202/204/206/ 207/208/227/228/229/231	Darlington	1925

All the above, commencing with Nos 4000-4009, later became LNER Nos 1800-1869, in the order they are listed.

Above: After the Grouping, Darlington built some 'K3s' to suit the loading gauge of the northern sections of the LNER. These had an even smaller chimney and dome, and a different cab design. The cab was basically of NER origin, with the windows set very low in the sides. (Later these windows were raised to a more conventional height). A new LNER 'group Standard' tender was fitted, also of somewhat NER appearance. No 69 is seen here in the original condition of the Darlington batch. *Ian Allan Library*

Centre left: Another Darlington-built 'K3', No 159, showing the cab windows raised to more conventional height. The engine was photographed on the turntable at Doncaster. The valve motion on the 'K3s' was kept as light as possible by the use of alloy steel rods, very finely machined. This and the use of a three-bar slidebar and light crosshead (a Gresley feature which first appeared on these engines) gave the 'K3s' an elegant appearance below the running plate. *T. G. Hepburn*

Bottom left: No 4006 (originally 1006) of the first GNR batch of 'K3s', but attached to an LNER 'Group Standard' tender, in place of the original. Photographed at Doncaster, 1928. In 1939 the 10 original engines had their GNR pattern cabs replaced by the standard LNER side-window version. *T. G. Hepburn*

Above: No 61800, the pioneer of the 'K3' class is seen here in BR days, passing Sleaford Junction, Boston, with a freight train. The early-type 'Group Standard' tender attached had a capacity of 4,200gal and 7½ton of coal. *R. C. Riley*

Below: In 1936 Class K3 2-6-0 No 227 was fitted with an experimental electrical foam indicator, intended to give the enginemen warning of priming. The engine is seen with this device, at New England in June 1939. Another detail change made to the class is evident; namely the later style of lagging to the smokebox saddle, behind the outside steampipes. *J. P. Wilson*

Nos 1300/12/18/31/45/64 65/67/68/86/87/88/89/ 91/92/94/95/96/97/98	Doncaster	1929
Nos 2761-2769	Darlington	1930
Nos 1100/1/2/6/8/17/18/19 21/25/33/35/37/41/54/ 56/58/62/64/66	Armstrong Whitworth	1930
Nos 1302/4/8/10/24/06/2934 35/36/37	Armstrong Whitworth	1934
Nos 1325/32/33/39/1399/ 1307/22/2938/39/40	Robert Stephenson & Hawthorn	1934/35
Nos 2425/26/27/28/38/39/40	North British	1935

42/43/47/48/49/50/51/ 59/61/63/66/67/68	North British	1935
Nos 2417/29/45/46/53/55/ 58/65/71/72	Armstrong Whitworth	1936
Nos 2470/73/98/99/3813-3832	Darlington	1936/37

All the above later became LNER Nos 1870-1992, in the order they are listed.

A final locomotive, which would have become No 3833, was cancelled and replaced by the first 'K4' for the West Highland line (see Section 23).

Following LNER practice the class was allocated part numbers, to distinguish tender types, springing modifications and weight distribution. In later LNER days these were as follows:

K3 Nos 1800-1809
K3/2 Nos 1810-1869
K3/3 Nos 1870-1889
K3/4 Nos 1890-1898
K3/5 Nos 1899-1915
K3/6 Nos 1916-1992

The 'K3' class was an undoubted asset to the LNER motive power stud, and proved popular for use on most kinds of work, including express passenger turns. On such trains speeds of 76mph or more were observed, and with loads of approximately 500 tons they could average roughly a mile a minute over the Kings Cross to Peterborough section.

If there was a drawback to the 'K3' class it must be admitted that they were rather large engines for their duties, with a consequent restriction upon their overall route availability. The adhesion weight on the three coupled axles was 60 tons. Their work on the routes open to them was excellent to the very end of their careers, and despite the indifferent maintenance of early postwar days some examples survived in BR ownership until the end of 1962. The livery of the 'K3' class in LNER days was black, and only one carried the postwar apple green livery; this

was No 1935, painted at Doncaster in 1947. In BR days they carried the mixed-traffic livery of black lined LNWR-style with red, cream and grey. One 'K3', No 206, was rebuilt as a two-cylinder engine by Thompson in 1945, becoming Class K5.

Last of class withdrawn: 61985 (1962)
None preserved

The basic dimensions of the class (in LNER days) were as follows:

Heating surfaces, tubes
   Large and small: 1,719sq ft
   Firebox: 182sq ft
Total (evaporative): 1,901sq ft
Superheater: 407sq ft
   Combined heating surfaces: 2,308sq ft
   Superheater elements: 32
Grate area: 28sq ft
Tractive effort (at 85 per cent BP): 30,031lb

Below: The imposing boiler and front end dimensions of Gresley's K3 Mogul are particularly well portrayed in this photograph of No 61868, taken as the engine left Sheffield Victoria on an up stopping train for Nottingham, in August 1958. *K. R. Pirt*

2-8-0 (3-cyl) GNR Class 02, LNER Class 02, BR Power Class 8F
Heavy Goods Engines
Introduced: 1921
Total: 66

It was a logical step to apply the refined conjugate valve gear, first used on the 'K3' Moguls, to a 2-8-0 type. The prototype three-cylinder engine had demonstrated its abilities when compared with the two-cylinder Class 01, and when further heavy freight engines became necessary in 1920/21, Gresley opted for an improved three-cylinder design. Compared to No 461, these engines had an increase in boiler pressure, from 170 to 180lb per sq in and the cylinder diameter was enlarged to 18½in. The front end layout closely resembled the three-cylinder Moguls, in having the three steam-chests in line, the middle cylinder being steeply inclined, with the valves operated by the two-to-one motion.

As in the case of the Moguls, the first of these engines featured the hallowed Doncaster cab and tender design, so that once again the front end looked more modern than the rest of the engine. The contract for the first ten was placed with the North British Locomotive Company, in April 1920 and they were delivered the following year.

With the Grouping the class became a new LNER standard for more widespread use, and construc-

tion continued steadily, as detailed below. The later batches from 1932 onwards received an enlarged side-window cab, and 'Group Standard' 4,200 gallon tenders, although some later ones were delivered new attached to reconditioned tenders of GCR origin.

One drawback of the three-cylinder engines was readily apparent during the World War 2 years, namely that they required more maintenance to keep them in superior form to the two-cylinder types (which they undoubtedly were, when in good trim). R. A. Riddles recalls that, early in the war, Gresley came to him and offered him a quantity of the 'O2s' for immediate war use overseas, on the basis that the Ministry of Supply would build a like number to replace them on the LNER. Riddles refused the offer, on the grounds that the machines were too refined for the job, and he chose the simpler Stanier two-cylinder LMSR 2-8-0 design instead.

The engines were built as follows:

Nos 477-486	North British (Atlas)	1921
Nos 487-501	Doncaster	1923/24
Nos 2954-2961	Doncaster	1932
Nos 2430-2437	Doncaster	1933
Nos 3833-3857	Doncaster	1942/3

Nos 477-501 become LNER Nos 3477-3501. Then in 1946 Nos 3477-3857 (ie *all* the above engines, in same order) became Nos 3922-3987.

Thompson fitted some engines with his type 100A boiler (designed for the 'B1' class 4-6-0) from 1943 onwards and these were classified as 'O2/4'. The other classifications related to overall height: 'O2/1', 'O2/2'; and side window cab and 'Group Standard' tender: 'O2/3'.

When Edward Thompson took charge of LNER locomotive affairs he decided to adopt a two-cylinder design for future standardisation (rebuilt from Robinson's GCR 2-8-0s) rather than the Gresley type.

Below: The drawing depicts the LNER standard version of the 'O2' class, with side-window cab and 'Group Standard' tender.

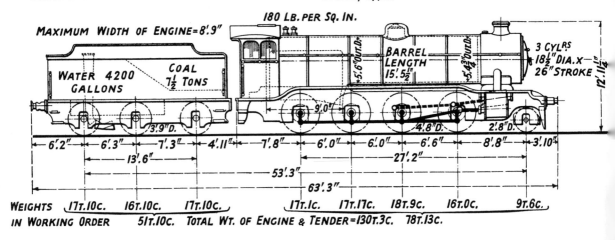

46

Above: No 483 of the first North British-built batch of 10 engines, delivered in 1921. Finished in GNR goods grey livery. As with the Moguls, the front end presented a more modern appearance than the rest of the engine, which retained the traditional GNR style. *C. L. Turner*

Below: Class O2 No 3480 (GNR No 480) at the head of an up 'C' class goods train at Brookmans Park, some time in the 1930s. These early engines, classified 'O2/1', were built to the full GNR loading gauge. *Photomatic*

Last of class withdrawn: Nos 63924/49/75/81/4 (1963)
None preserved

The basic dimensions (to LNER standard) of the engines were as follows:

Heating surface, tubes
  Large and small: 1,868.5sq ft
  Firebox: 163.5sq ft
Total (evaporative): 2,032sq ft
Superheater: 430.5sq ft

Combined heating surfaces: 2,462.5sq ft
Superheater elements: 24
Grate area: 27.5sq ft
Tractive effort (at 85 per cent BP): 36,470lb

Below: No 3500, delivered from Doncaster in May 1924, ran for some time with an experimental Dabeg feedwater heater (fitted in 1925), as seen here. Note the crank drive from the rear coupled wheels. These post-Grouping 'O2s' had the overall height reduced, and a smaller chimney. The cab roof was more rounded in cross-section. *Ian Allan Library*

Left: Starting in 1932 the new engines built had side-window cabs and 'Group Standard' tenders, but the wartime engines (built 1942/43) had tin sheets instead of glass panes, as an air raid precaution, and some such as No 3834 seen here, were attached to reconditioned GCR tenders, taken from the 'Q4' class. *British Rail ER*

Above: No 63946, in BR black goods engine livery; one of the batch built at Doncaster in 1924, and still retaining the GNR style cab and tender. At the head of a coal train during the 1950s. *Eric Treacy*

Above: Class O2/4, rebuilt with a Thompson type 100A boiler, as used on his 'B1' class 4-6-0s. This was shorter, and necessitated a distance piece between the boiler and the existing smokebox, as can be clearly seen in this ex-works shot of No 63932. The engine has received a side-window cab in place of the GNR style original, but it is still attached to a GNR type tender. Photographed at March in June 1956. *G. Wheeler*

Below: Running light engine, Class O2/3 2-8-0 No 63962 was photographed near Essendine in June 1963. The 'O2/3' variation had the flush-sided version of the LNER 'Group Standard' 4,200gal tender, and these engines were built new with side window cabs. *P. H. Wells*

SECTION 8

0-6-2T GNR Class N2, LNER Class N2, BR Power Class 3MT
Passenger Tank Engines
Introduced: 1920
Total: 107

The spread of population from the centre of London to what purported to be the peace and tranquillity of the new suburban avenues of the Northern Heights, was a major source of business for the GNR. Gresley designed his articulated non-corridor suburban carriages specifically to carry the morning and evening migrants, and there was every indication that this particular traffic would continue to flourish. Part of the service operated to the heart of the City via the Metropolitan lines, below street level. For this reason it was desirable to have engines fitted with condensing gear, to reduce the amount of exhaust released into the tunnels.

By 1919 it was considered necessary to produce a more powerful type of locomotive for this suburban traffic, and Doncaster began drawing up some schemes to Gresley's requirements. To begin with they were a shade too ambitious; first producing a 2-6-2T with three cylinders and then a 2-6-4T, but it was realised that a smaller engine would have to suffice. One problem was the very restricted layout at Moorgate station, which governed the length of a train plus engine. The final solution arrived at was a modernised and enlarged version of the Ivatt Class N1 0-6-2Ts, already operating the service. This new design was Gresley's inside-cylinder 'N2' class 0-6-2T of 1920.

Compared to the Ivatt engines, the 'N2s' had larger diameter cylinders, 19in by 26in, with piston valves, and they were superheated. Their appearance was massive, the high-pitched 170lb per sq in boiler (necessary to clear the piston valves above

the cylinders) being matched with a very short chimney, because of the restricted Metropolitan line loading gauge. Sixty engines were ordered in 1920, all fitted with condensing gear, and the LNER perpetuated the design as a 'Group Standard', building some without condensing gear for use in Scotland; these later engines had left-hand drive. The engines were built as follows:

GNR Nos 1606-1615	Doncaster	1920/21
GNR Nos 1721-1770	North British	1920/21
LNER Nos 2583-2594	Beyer, Peacock	1925
LNER Nos 892-897	Doncaster	1925
LNER Nos 2662-2681	Hawthorn, Leslie	1928/29
LNER Nos 2682-2684	Yorkshire Engine Co	1928
LNER Nos 2685-2690	Yorkshire Engine Co	1928/29

The LNER renumbered the GNR engines as Nos 4606-4615 and Nos 4721-4770; these later became Nos 9490-9499 and 9500-9561 respectively. Nos 892-897 became Nos 9562-9567; Nos 2662-2690 became Nos 9568-9596. BR added 60000 to the numbers.

The 1925 batch, Nos 892-897, were dual-fitted with vacuum and Westinghouse brakes, for the Scottish area, and they were not condensing engines. In the course of their careers some engines were converted to operate as condensing engines, or vice versa, and some received air brakes. The Scottish engines had taller chimneys, but some received short ones when transferred to the South. The part numbers allocated to the class referred mainly to whether they were condensing engines or not,

Below: Class N2 0-6-2T, with condensing gear; in LNER standard condition.

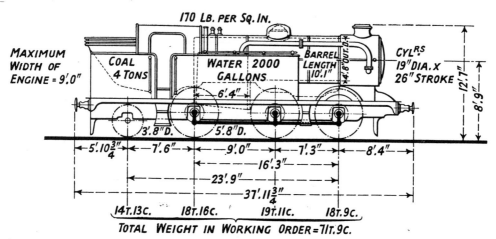

Above: The classic view of a Gresley GNR 'N2' class 0-6-2T at work, coupled to two sets of his 'quad-art' non-corridor articulated suburban carriages. Here No 1730 heads the down 5.0pm to Cambridge past New Southgate in 1921; it carries the headboard 'Main Line', and is evidently going along in very fine style indeed. This view shows the horizontal handrail which was at first located on the side of the side tanks, but later moved to a position on top of the tanks. *H. Gordon Tidey*

Below: Fresh from the maker, No 1757, built by the North British Locomotive Company in March 1921 and seen at Kings Cross in the Spring of that year, waits to leave on a suburban working. Note the locomotive number just visible, painted on the rear of the bunker, above the destination board. Because of the loading gauge restriction the cutaway of the top of the cab entrance had to be curved into the cab roof instead of ending at a more conventional gutter line. Horizontal handrail to tank moved from the side to a position above. *A. B. MacLeod*

except for part 'N2/4' which referred to Nos 9568-9593 which were slightly heavier engines.

The GNR engines were painted in the full passenger green livery, but in LNER days the livery was black with red lining. After World War 2 one engine, No 9522, was painted apple green, but the rest of the class remained black, receiving the LNWR style lining in BR days. All the class passed into BR ownership, and they were still performing the same sort of duties that Gresley had designed them for. They were excellent engines, with an outstanding performance for their size, and it was only the coming of the diesels that ousted them from the Kings Cross suburban services, on which they reigned for up to forty years. Late in life the remaining examples were used in other areas, including the Great Eastern section.

Last of class withdrawn: 69504/20/9/46/68/75/9/83/ 93 (1962)
Example preserved: 69523 (LNER 4744)

The basic dimensions of the class, in LNER days, were as follows:

Heating surface, tubes
  Large and small: 880sq ft
  Firebox: 118sq ft
Total (evaporative): 998sq ft
Superheater: 207sq ft
  Combined heating surfaces: 1,205sq ft
  Superheater elements: 17
Grate area: 19sq ft
Tractive effort (at 85 per cent BP): 19,945lb

Below: Full GNR passenger green livery sits prettily on the form of Class N2 0-6-2T No 1763, also photographed when it had just arrived, brand new from the builder, the North British Locomotive Co Ltd. Because of the restricted loading gauge on the Metropolitan lines, these engines were only 12ft 7in high overall, giving them a squat but massive appearance. *Ian Allan Library*

Below: The 892 series of 'N2' class 0-6-2Ts was constructed at Doncaster in 1925, being classified 'N2/3'. These engines had improved axleboxes and springing, and had Westinghouse brakes in addition to vacuum braking. No condensing gear was fitted, or ever carried by this particular series. No 897 is seen here in shop grey livery, for photographic purposes, but the engines were delivered to traffic in the LNER black livery, with red lining. *LPC*

Bottom: The condensing gear that Gresley used on the 'N2s' gave a certain amount of trouble in everyday use, and in 1927 it was suggested that the alternative type of gear used on the GER-type 'N7s', built at Doncaster under Gresley's direction, should be tried out instead. Hawthorn Leslie, who were building the batch, fitted it new to Nos 2673-2684, as seen here, and the earlier ones of the batch, Nos 2662-2672, were altered similarly at Doncaster after delivery. Noticeable is the absence of the U-bend in the pipe; the change in design did not prove to be very satisfactory. Photographed in shop grey livery is No 2684, the last of the class to be built, in 1929. *LPC*

Above: No 2676 of the 2662 series seen working a down class 'C' goods at Hatfield in 1937. This was a left-hand drive engine, a change first made with the 2583 series, to suit the standard LNER practice. The GNR design featured right-hand drive, and the engines built to that company's orders were never altered. *Photomatic*

Below: No 2592 of the 2583 series, without condensing gear, and with left hand drive; showing its paces to the camera in Princes Street Gardens, Edinburgh, in 1935. These engines had a taller chimney than those that were required to operate over the Metropolitan lines in London. *Photomatic*

Above: Once a familiar sight at Moorgate during the morning and evening rush hours was this gathering of London Transport electrics, plus Eastern Region 'N2s' with Gresley's articulated suburban stock, and London Midland Region Fowler 2-6-2Ts. The steam locomotives carried condensing gear to reduce exhaust emissions whilst working through the LT tunnels. 'N2' No 69576 is seen leaving for New Barnet on 30 July, 1958. *R. C. Riley*

Centre right: Smartly turned out in lined black livery, with the style of lettering which preceded the first BR lion and wheel totem. No 69580 leaves Kings Cross suburban platforms for Hertford. This particular engine was turned out in this style to participate in an exhibition at Doncaster works in July 1948. *Ian Allan Library*

Bottom right: No 69530 seen here at Stratford works, gleamingly fresh from a general repair in November 1954. The BR lined black livery has been augmented by the use of single red lining on the leading sandbox and splashers; a feature of LNER days. *G. Wheeler*

SECTION 9

4-6-2 (3-cyl) GNR Class A1, LNER Class A1 (later A10)
Express Passenger Engines
Introduced: 1922
Total: 52

The heavy passenger train loads of the World War I years, sometimes as many as 15-17 carriages, had taxed the large-boilered Ivatt Atlantics to their very limits. Gresley had already seen the need to obtain engines of greater power and adhesion for the future, and had commenced planning such engines, by 1915. The first practical result of this was the appearance in traffic of his large-boilered three-cylinder Mogul, the 'H4' (LNER Class K3), in 1920. It was the success of these engines when put to work on heavy passenger trains during the 1921 coal strike, that demonstrated so convincingly the need for a six-coupled engine for future main line passenger power. Also, the wide firebox and grate of the Moguls had shown itself capable of steaming well, even on the inferior quality foreign coal that the engines were forced to burn at this time.

Any remaining doubts that may have existed in Gresley's mind must have been dispelled by these events, and so the tentative schemes for a 2-6-2, which had followed on from the original 1915 proposal for a four-cylinder Pacific, were put aside in favour of a large-boilered three-cylinder Pacific design, which would meet the Civil Engineers' requirements for axle loads and would utilise the GNR loading gauge to the full. It seems that Gresley had studied locomotive developments in America with some interest, in particular the development of a taper boiler with combustion chambers by the Pennsylvania Railroad in 1916 for its famous 'K4' Pacific design. A similar taper boiler, but with round topped firebox and wide grate, could, he must have

realised, be scaled down to suit the British loading gauge. This boiler, with its firebox combustion chamber, could be shorter than the boiler he had planned for his 1915 Pacific, and the taper would allow better forward vision for the driver.

In the spring of 1922, Nigel Gresley's first Pacific locomotive, No 1470 *Great Northern,* was completed at Doncaster and sent to Kings Cross in April for exhibition. Even today we can visualise the profound impression this superb new engine must have made upon those seeing it for the first time. Gone were the last vestiges of GNR Victorian styling, and in their place was an aesthetically pleasing modern machine. The impression given by the sheer size of the engine, was matched by its good proportions and excellent workmanship. A spacious side-window cab, a large high-sided eight wheeled tender, the big tapered boiler and an extremely elegant arrangement for the nickel-chrome steel outside valve motion all added up to a masterpiece of locomotive engineering. A second engine, No 1471 (soon named *Sir Frederick Banbury*) appeared some three months later.

Great Northern was only the second Pacific locomotive to be built for a British railway, and it demonstrated a considerable technical and aesthetic advance over Churchward's pioneer *The Great Bear* of 1908, an engine which could be truthfully described as only a moderate success. Indeed the story goes that upon hearing of Gresley's new Pacific, Churchward in conversation with Holcroft said 'Why did that young man want to build a Pacific? We could have sold him ours!'

Below: Class A1 Pacific, as first introduced in April 1922 with boiler mountings and cab roof to GNR loading gauge. Tender shows the original front top corners.

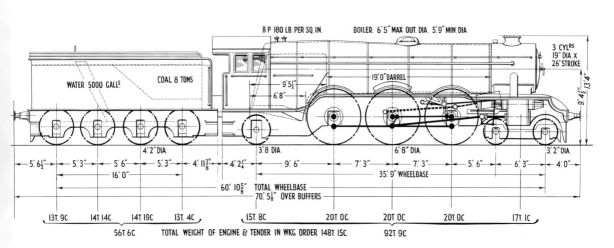

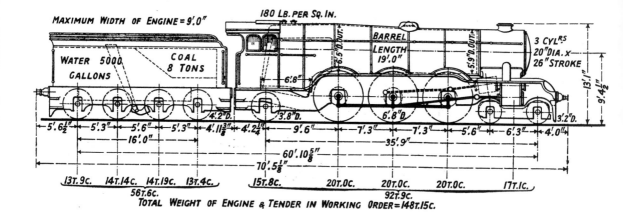

MAXIMUM WIDTH OF ENGINE = 9'.0"

180 LB. PER SQ. IN.

WATER 5000 GALLONS

COAL 8 TONS

BARREL LENGTH 19'.0"

3 CYL^RS 20"DIA. X 26" STROKE

13'.1"

9'.4½"

6'.8"

4'.2"D. 3'.8"D. 6'.8"D. 3'.2"D.

5'.6½" 5'.3" 5'.6" 5'.3" 4'.11¾" 4'.2¼" 9'.6" 7'.3" 7'.3" 5'.6" 6'.3" 4'.0"

16'.0"

35'.9"

60'.10⅝"

70'.5⅛"

13T.9C. 14T.14C. 14T.19C. 13T.4C. 15T.8C. 20T.0C. 20T.0C. 20T.0C. 17T.1C.

56T.6C.

92T.9C.

TOTAL WEIGHT OF ENGINE & TENDER IN WORKING ORDER=148T.15C.

Above: Class A1 Pacific; production series in LNER days. Height over boiler mountings reduced to 13ft 1in, with raised ventilator on cab roof.

Right: Elevation and plan of the eight-wheeled corridor tender design introduced in 1928 to allow non-stop running between London and Edinburgh.

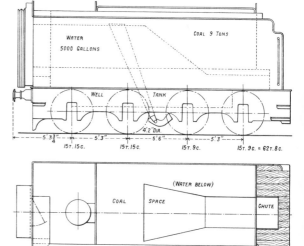

WATER 5000 GALLONS COAL 9 TONS

WELL TANK

4'.2" DIA.

5'.3¾" 5'.3" 5'.6" 5'.3"

15T.15C. 15T.15C. 15T.9C. 15T.9C. = 62T.8C.

(WATER BELOW)

COAL SPACE CHUTE

C O R R I D O R 18" WIDE X 5'.0" HIGH

Gresley's conjugated three-cylinder layout was used on the Pacific, very similar to the 'K3' arrangement except that the cylinders were of 20in diameter, and the piston valves were 8in diameter. Maximum cut-off was limited to 65 per cent, and the valve-travel to 4⁹/₁₆in, in order to reduce to a minimum any tendency for the valve gear of the centre cylinder to over-travel at high speeds. This had proved to be a troublesome feature with the Moguls, but by reducing the lap of the valves, Gresley unwittingly produced a handicap to the Pacific's initial performance. The boiler pressure was 180lb, which seemed adequate for the demands of the time.

The two engines quickly established their worth in everyday service, between Doncaster and London. Gresley himself claimed that they could handle loads of 600 tons to express timings and to prove this he organised a demonstration run from London to Grantham and back, with No 1471 hauling no less than 20 bogie coaches weighing 610 tons loaded. This ran to the current 'Flying Scotsman' timings, and No 1471 averaged 70mph on the levels between Hitchin and Huntingdon with this immense load, topping Stoke summit at 45mph. Not surprisingly the GNR ordered a further 10 of the class, once their abilities had been so clearly demonstrated.

These 10 locomotives were delivered to service after the Grouping, in 1923 and became LNER engines, although they carried their intended GNR numbers to begin with. As Gresley was appointed CME of the new railway company, it was only to be expected that he would begin to envisage a wider use for his new Pacifics. One obstacle to this was the fact that he had designed them to suit the generous GNR loading gauge. To use them in Northern and Scottish areas he had to reduce their height and improve their clearances at platform level. To put this to a practical test he had the last of these 10 locomotives altered during construction (see page 64), with a lower chimney, dome and modified cab roof.

First of this batch of 10 was No 1472 (later LNER No 4472) and this was selected by the LNER for exhibition at the 1924 Empire Exhibition at Wembley. For this occasion it was named *Flying Scotsman,* and with this distinctive name it was destined to become one of the most fabled engines of all time. The story of how the Gresley Pacific and the GWR Collett 'Castle' class 4-6-0 were exhibited

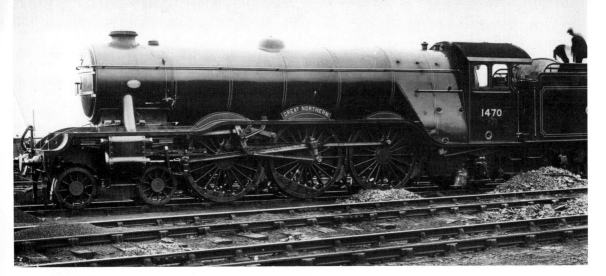

Top: Gresley's first Pacific, No 1470 *Great Northern,* in original 1922 condition, with high roof to cab and tall chimney and dome. Full passenger green livery was carried, with number painted on cabsides. The elegant valve motion was manufactured in nickel-chrome steel, to reduce weight without affecting the strength of the individual components. *Ian Allan Library*

Above: Class A1 Pacific No 1470 *Great Northern* at speed with a GNR main line passenger train, shortly before the 1923 Grouping. The two pioneer Pacifics soon demonstrated their ability to handle heavy loads to express passenger timings, and the GNR had 10 more on order when the 1923 Grouping took place; these were delivered as LNER engines (see page 58). *LPC*

together, at Wembley, with the GWR claiming that its engine was 'Britain's most powerful passenger locomotive', and of the subsequent exchange trials between the two classes over each other's routes, is too well known to warrant further repetition here.

What is important to our story is that the trials revealed a distinct superiority in the design of the long-travel valve gear on the Collett engines, and a resultant economy in coal consumption. As a result, Gresley's assistant Spencer finally persuaded his chief to fit an altered valve gear, with the long-travel valves that Gresley had dismissed to prevent over-riding of the middle cylinder valve, following experience with the 'K3s'. First of all a modification was made to the valve setting of No 4477 *Gay Crusader,* with some saving in fuel. Then a more complete redesign of the valve gear was drawn up and this modification was made to No 2555 *Centenary,* stationed at Doncaster and therefore easy to keep under observation.

Compared to a 'standard' Pacific, No 2559, *Centenary,* on the Doncaster-London run showed a reduction in coal consumption on a round trip from about 50lb per mile to about 40lb per mile. Once

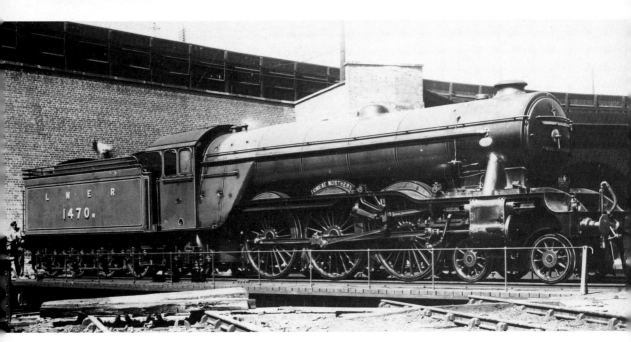

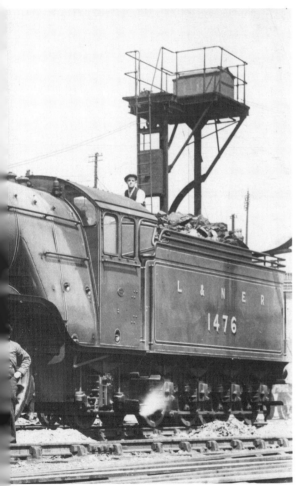

Top left: Early days in LNER ownership, with the new initials on the tender, and with the number transferred from cabside to tender side. The sectional suffix N has been added to the existing GNR number. Shortly after this the LNER added 3000 to the GNR numbers and No 1470N *Great Northern* then became No 4470. Photographed on the turntable at Kings Cross in 1923. *Ian Allan Library*

Left: Coaling-up at Kings Cross yard is No 1476 (the intended GNR number, although it never ran in that railway's ownership). As yet unnamed, this engine became LNER No 4476 *Royal Lancer*. Note the ampersand used with the initials on the tender (L & NER); this was only carried for the first few months in traffic. These 10 engines, ordered by the GNR, appeared from Doncaster in the period February-July 1923, after the Grouping and were numbered 1472-1481, later becoming Nos 4472-4481. All but the last one were built to the generous GNR loading gauge; the last one, No 4481, had the chimney height and diameter reduced and the cab roof modified (see page 58). Front footstep fitted and bufferbeam not cutaway at corners. *LPC*

Above: Class A1 Pacific No 4471 *Flying Scotsman* on exhibition at Wembley, for the Centenary of British railways in 1925; attached to a green liveried Class K3 tender because of limited space. This was the second year that No 4472 had been exhibited at Wembly, and it had received its name specially for the 1924 Empire Exhibition. Special features were the polished brass beadings to the coupled wheel splashers and the LNER coat of arms on the cabsides. Front footstep fitted. *H. C. Casserley collection*

Gresley had convinced himself of the superiority of No 2555 he had the order issued for all engines to be similarly altered. Visually the modification can be spotted in photographs by the wider and elongated flat-topped casing on the running plate, around the outside steampipes. All the 'A1s' were fitted with long-travel valves by mid-1931 and the cost of this alteration was well recompensed by the savings in fuel achieved.

A further 40 Class A1 Pacifics were ordered by the LNER for delivery in 1924-25, with 20 each being built by Doncaster and the North British Locomotive Company. These engines were built to the reduced loading gauge, and Nos 2568-82 were dual-fitted, with the Westinghouse brake and vacuum, for service in the North-Eastern Area. These also had Raven's patent fog signalling apparatus when new.

The engines were built as follows:

GNR Nos 1470/1	Doncaster	1922
LNER Nos 1472-1481	Doncaster	1923
LNER Nos 2543-2562	Doncaster	1924/25
LNER Nos 2563-2582	North British	1924

Nos 1470-1481 were soon renumbered Nos 4470-4481 by the LNER. For a short period in 1946 the following engines received new numbers (shown in brackets) before the second 1946 renumbering scheme: Nos 4472 (502), 4477 (507), 4478 (508), 4481 (511), 2548 (517), 2549 (518), 2550 (519), 2551 (520), 2552 (521), 2553 (522), 2559 (528), 2562 (531), 2568 (537), 2569 (538), 2573 (542), 2576 (545).

In the second 1946 renumbering scheme the following changes were made (new numbers in brackets): No 4470 (113), Nos 4471-4481 (102-112), Nos 2543-2582 (44-83). BR added 60000 to these numbers in 1948.

Below: Following exhibition of an 'A1' Pacific and a GWR 'Castle' class 4-6-0 at the 1924 Wembley Empire Exhibition, the GWR sent No 4079 *Pendennis Castle* to the LNER in 1925 to compete with Class A1 Pacific No 4475 *Flying Fox,* over the East Coast main line. No 4475 ran hot on the first day, and No 2545 was substituted on the second day. On average the Pacific burned 3.7lb of coal per mile more than the 'Castle' class 4-6-0. *Flying Fox* and *Pendennis Castle* are seen here posed for the camera at Top Shed, Kings Cross. It was a direct outcome of these trials that alterations were made to the valve gear of the Pacifics, and then higher-pressure boilers fitted, thereby producing the 'A3' class (see Section 15). *LPC*

The engines built to the GNR gauge were classified 'A1/1' by the LNER, and the reduced dimension engines were classified 'A1/2'. All the 'A1/1' versions were altered to 'A1/2' dimensions by 1933.

These engines were built with right-hand drive, and although a request was made by the Running Department in 1932 for their conversion to left-hand

Top: The 'Cornish Riviera Limited' passing Hayes in the charge of Class A1 Pacific No 4474 (unnamed) during the 1925 locomotive exchange between the LNER and the GWR. No 4474 was a substitute for No 4475 which had developed a hot box, and therefore did not go to Old Oak Common shed. The GWR selected its No 4074 *Caldicot Castle* to compete with the Gresley engine on the Plymouth route. The 'Castle' burned an average of 6lb of coal per mile less than the Pacific. *F. R. Hebron*

Above: Still retaining the polished brass splasher beading, and the cabside coat of arms, No 4472 *Flying Scotsman* is seen here at Grantham shed in 1927, with its own original tender attached. At this time the engine was fitted with a variable blastpipe, and the operating rod and crank for this can be seen running along the boiler side to the smokebox. Front footstep removed. *T. G. Hepburn*

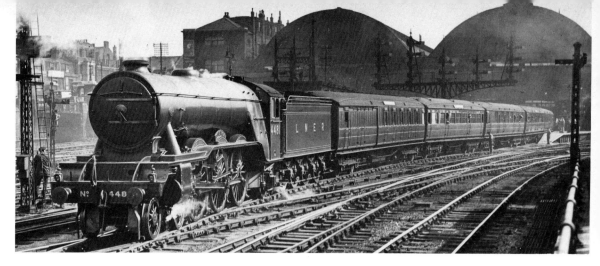

Above: No 4481 *St. Simon,* last of the batch of 10 locomotives delivered from Doncaster as No 1481, in 1923, was altered during construction to conform to the more restricted NBR loading gauge. This was a logical move, as Gresley envisaged wider use of his new Pacifics over the lines of the newly-formed LNER. The chimney height was reduced, and the shape altered, a lower dome and safety valves were fitted and the cab roof was lowered, leaving the ventilator projecting above it. The lower corners of the front bufferbeam were cut away and the front footstep was removed. No 4481 is seen here leaving Kings Cross at the head of the 4.0pm to Newcastle, and this picture was taken after the engine had been altered to long-travel valve gear, as is evidenced by the enlarged casing over the cylinders at the base of the outside steampipe. *A. P. Reavil*

Below: In 1923 a further 40 Class A1 Pacifics were ordered; 20 from Doncaster and 20 from North British, being delivered in 1924/25. These were built to the reduced NBR loading gauge, and their smaller boiler mountings somehow gave them a more massive appearance. No 2559 *The Tetrarch,* built at Doncaster in 1925, is seen here working the 5.45pm to Harrogate, passing Potters Bar. Still fitted with the original short-travel valves, and with right-hand drive. *F. R. Hebron*

drive, this modification did not take place until the 1950s, under BR auspices.

When the idea of running a train non-stop from London to Edinburgh was brought to fruition in 1928 (a move made possible by the reduced fuel consumption of the long-travel valve engines), Gresley decided against the idea of having two crews travelling on one footplate. Instead, he devised a corridor tender (see page 58) whereby the relief crew could travel in the comfort of the train and then make their way forward to the footplate, via the corridor tender. Ten new tenders were built that year, at Doncaster, to ensure there was always a tender available as a spare.

In 1927, following some superheater experiments with the Class A1 180lb boilers, Gresley decided to fit boilers of the higher pressure of 220lb to five engines. The first to receive one of these boilers was No 4480 *Enterprise,* and the story of this and the subsequent development of the 'A3' class, as it

Above: Class A1 4-6-2 No 2582 *Sir Hugo,* working the 10.5am from Kings Cross, in 1930. This was one of the North British Locomotive Company batch, of which 15 were allocated to the North Eastern Area and fitted (as seen here) with the Westinghouse brake; a feature they carried until 1933-34. By the time this picture was taken the engine had been modified with long-travel valves. *A. P. Reavil*

Left: The first London-Edinburgh non-stop express leaving Kings Cross on 1 May 1928 behind engine No 4472 *Flying Scotsman,* fitted with a new corridor tender, and modified with long-travel valves, but retaining 180lb boiler pressure. Boiler mountings and cab reduced in height and lower corners of front bufferbeam cut away. *Ian Allan Library*

Above: Class A1 No 4476 *Royal Lancer,* the other of the two London-based engines originally fitted with a corridor tender for the London-Edinburgh non-stop workings. Also fitted with long-travel valves and with boiler mountings and cab height reduced. The following Class A1 Pacifics ran with corridor tenders at some time: Nos 2546/7/52/63-6/9, 4472-6. *LPC*

Centre right: The down 3.40pm express goods seen near Ganwick in September 1937 in the charge of Class A1 Pacific No 2561 *Minoru;* fitted with long-travel valves, and with later style non-corridor tender. *M. W. Earley*

Bottom right: Still running as a Class A1 Pacific, with 180lb boiler pressure, but with long-travel valves and cut down height, No 4473 *Solario* is seen here at Nottingham Victoria in June 1939, on a through Manchester-Marylebone working. Front footsteps fitted, with solid backplates, and lower corners of bufferbeam cutaway. Speedometer drive taken from rear coupled wheels. *J. F. Henton.*

became known, is related in Section 15. Conversion of the 'A1' engines to Class A3 was steadily pursued by the LNER, and no more 'A1' type boilers were built after 1925. The last engine to be converted was No 68 *Sir Visto* in December 1948. By this time the few remaining 180lb boiler pressure engines had been reclassified 'A10' by Thompson, to make way for his own new Class A1 Pacifics.

A sad note on which to end the Class A1 story is the rebuilding by Thompson of Gresley's pioneer engine *Great Northern,* in 1945, as a singularly ugly locomotive with three independent sets of Walschaerts valve gear. This locomotive is described in Appendix Two.

All the Class A1 Pacifics, except No 4470 *Great Northern* were rebuilt as Class A3s, and their subsequent history is dealt with in Section 15.

The basic dimensions of the LNER standard engines were as follows:

Heating surface, tubes
 Large and small: 2,715.0sq ft
 Firebox: 215.0sq ft
Total (evaporative): 2,930.0sq ft
Superheaters: 525.0sq ft
 Combined heating surfaces: 3,455.0sq ft
 Superheater elements: 32
Grate area: 41.25sq ft
Tractive effort (at 85 per cent BP): 29,835lb

Locomotives for the LNER 1923 – 1941

SECTION 10

2-8-2 (3-cyl) LNER Class P1
Heavy Mineral Engines
Introduced: 1925
Total: 2

Gresley, alone of all the British CMEs, used the 2-8-2 or Mikado wheel arrangement, which was a very popular one in North America and on the Continent. His first Mikados were two massive engines, and they were his first new design to appear after the Grouping, when he became CME of the new LNER. Their purpose was to haul 100-wagon 1,600ton coal trains between Peterborough and Ferme Park, Hornsey, and for this reason they spent their entire lives allocated to New England shed, Peterborough.

Basically their boiler design was the same as that of the first Gresley Pacifics which they closely resembled in many other respects, but this fed steam to a booster unit as well as to the cylinders. The booster engine drove on to trailing wheels beneath the cab, and had two 10in by 12in cylinders, which when in operation, provided an extra 9,000lb of tractive effort. The booster was mainly employed when starting a train away from a stand, or when climbing gradients.

The two engines, Nos 2393/4, were built at Doncaster in 1925. It seems that the design was an experiment made at the request of the Operating Department, and although the engines themselves showed that the 1,600ton loads were quite within their capabilities, these lengthy trains proved to be something of a headache for the operators, because they were too long to go into some of the loops on the GN main line. When new, the engines were both fitted with the Westinghouse brake. After a while the loads were reduced to a maximum of 92 wagons and the booster engines were not used so much. An Operating Department change of policy then placed the emphasis upon running shorter, faster trains, hauled by Gresley's 'K3' Moguls, and the two Mikados were out of the limelight. When the boosters became due for cylinder renewal round about 1938 they were removed from both locomotives, because by that time they were seldom used. The Westinghouse brakes were also removed.

When Gresley was considering the use of the 2-8-2 wheel arrangement for express passenger work on the Edinburgh-Aberdeen main line, he arranged for No 2394 to haul the 7.45am Kings Cross-Peterborough semi-fast passenger turn, and the big freight engine reached a speed of 65mph en route. The other notable moment in their careers was right at the start, when No 2393 was exhibited in brand new condition at the 1925 Railway Centenary event at Darlington.

During World War 2, in 1942/3, the two engines received boilers similar to the 220lb type used on the 'A3' Pacifics (see Section 15) and the cylinders were reduced to 19in diameter. Just how this affected their performance does not appear to have been recorded, but it is interesting to note that in their original condition they were considered to be quite difficult engines for the fireman to handle. Their fate was sealed when Edward Thompson succeeded Gresley, and both were withdrawn from service in July 1945.

Below: Class P1 2-8-2, with booster fitted, and special 4,700gal tender.

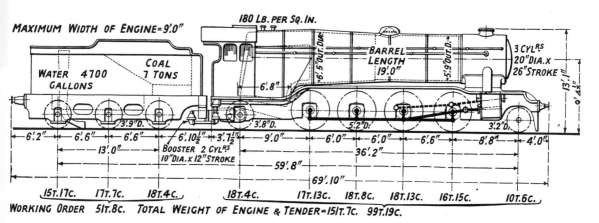

67

None preserved

The basic dimensions of the class with original boilers were as follows:

Heating surface, tubes
   Large and small: 2,715.0sq ft
   Firebox: 215.0sq ft
Total (evaporative): 2,930.0sq ft
Superheater: 525.0sq ft
   Combined heating surfaces: 3,455.0sq ft
   Superheater elements: 32
Grate area: 41.25sq ft
Tractive effort (at 85 per cent BP): 38,500lb*

(*Increased to 47,500lb with booster in operation)

Right: Class P1 2-8-2 No 2394, in original condition, with booster fitted to the trailing wheel beneath the cab, and with Westinghouse brake pump on the boiler side. The livery was black with red lining; changed to plain black during the war. Twin Gresley anti-vacuum valves behind chimney, carried while the engine was fitted with a 62-element 'E' type superheater as an experiment. A similar superheater was fitted to Class A1 Pacific No 2562 *Isinglass* in 1926. *LPC*

Below: A mighty Mikado in full cry, as No 2394 breasts the summit at Potters Bar with a 100-wagon trainload, and with the booster engine in operation. The big boiler and small chimney gave these two engines a very impressive appearance. *F. R. Hebron*

Bottom right: No 2393 at New England shed in June 1939, after removal of the booster and air brakes. Single Gresley anti-vacuum valve behind the chimney. During the Second World War both engines received boilers similar to those used on the 'A3' class, with 220lb per sq in pressure and banjo domes. *J. P. Wilson*

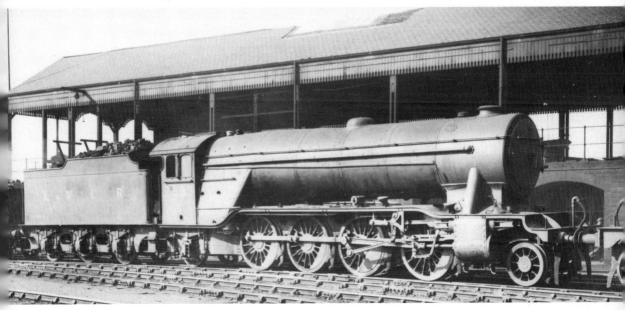

SECTION 11

2-8-0 + 0-8-2T (6-cyl) LNER Class U1
Banking Engine
Introduced: 1925
Total: 1

A unique locomotive in several respects, the solitary Beyer-Garratt engine built for the LNER in 1925 was the most powerful steam locomotive ever to see service in Great Britain. It was completed in time to be exhibited at the Railway Centenary celebrations at Darlington, where its massive dimensions must have created quite a stir. The engine was intended for use as a banking engine, on the Worsborough incline, between Wentworth Junction and West Silkstone Junction; a route used by heavy coal trains.

It seems that as far back as 1910, the Great Central Railway had given some thought to the construction of a Garratt type locomotive, and at the time of the Grouping this idea was still in the air. The LNER very soon approached Beyer, Peacock & Co Ltd for an outline drawing and quotation, for the supply of two such engines. The two-times-two cylinder layout, based upon the GCR Robinson standard 2-8-0 was suggested for the engine part.

It was entirely in keeping with Gresley's contemporary work on large three-cylinder engines that he should next decide that the proposed Garratt should have three cylinders, instead of two, and that as much of the valve motion as was possible (because of a different wheel spacing) was to match the layout of his '02' class 2-8-0s, instead of the earlier Robinson engines, only one engine was ordered, to Gresley's amended design. The Beyer, Peacock boiler had a round-top firebox, Robinson

Below: Class U1 Gresley/Garratt locomotive.

superheater and twin Gresley anti-vacuum valves. A steam reverser was fitted.

The engine was built at Gorton by Beyer, Peacock, in 1925.

As a banking engine the Garratt proved very effective, replacing two engines and two men, and making some 18 trips in the course of a day. As with all such large engines, the fireman had a tough time of it, and it could be argued that he was actually having to perform a task normally the lot of two men on two footplates.

With the electrification of the Manchester-Sheffield-Wath line (the delayed prewar LNER scheme) in 1949, the Garratt was no longer needed for Worsborough incline. The boiler was due for renewal at about the same time, and to justify this BR looked for suitable alternative employment for the engine. The Lickey incline, of 1 in 37.7 was chosen—on the LMR Birmingham-Bristol main line—and the Garratt was sent to Bromsgrove shed. It did not prove popular with the LMR men. There then followed periods of store, and some further use on the Eastern Region, before it was decided to convert the engine to oil-firing and return it to Bromsgrove. Even this failed to gain popularity for the engine, and it was withdrawn from service at the end of 1955.

Not preserved

The principal dimensions of the engine, as built, were as follows:

Heating surface, tubes
    Large and small: 2,644.5sq ft
    Firebox: 223.5sq ft
Total (evaporative): 2,868.0sq ft
Superheater: 650.0sq ft
    Combined heating surfaces: 3,518.0sq ft
    Superheater elements: 45
Grate area: 56.5sq ft
Tractive effort (at 85 per cent BP): 72.940lb

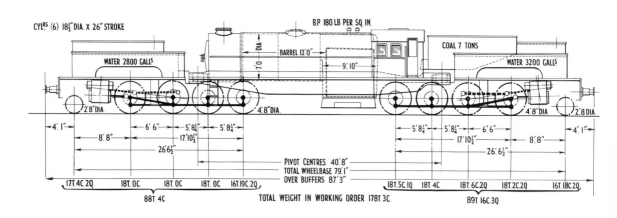

Above: Still in the maker's workshop grey livery, No 2395 was exhibited at the 1925 Railway Centenary event at Darlington. Construction was specially hurried for this occasion, and Beyer, Peacock completed the locomotive in 21 days. After exhibition the engine was sent to Doncaster to receive the standard black livery.
P. Ransome-Wallis

Below: Renumbered as No 9999, the unique Class U1 Garratt is seen here at Wentworth Junction in April 1947. This is where it spent the major part of its career, banking coal trains up the Worsborough incline to West Silkstone Junction. It was displaced from this job by electrification.
H. C. Casserley

Above: An alternative job for the Garratt was found by British Railways in 1949/50, when it was sent to work as a banking engine on the LMR Bristol-Birmingham line, at Lickey. It is seen here at Blackwell in May 1949, renumbered No 69999 and with the words 'British Railways' painted along the sides of the frames of the engine portion, beneath the boiler. *H. C. Casserley*

Below: The engine was fitted with oil-firing at Gorton in 1952, and a steam-driven generator (visible on the side of the smokebox) was fitted to power a large electric headlight on the bunker end. After various trials and some modifications, it was again sent to Lickey, in 1955, but it did not prove a success as an oil-burner and it was condemned in December the same year. No 69999 is seen standing dead at Burton-on-Trent, en route to Doncaster for breaking-up. *F. Spencer Yeates*

SECTION 12

0-6-0 LNER Class J38, BR Power Class 6F Goods Engines
Introduced: 1926
Total: 35

When an urgent need for greater motive power arose on the North British Section of the LNER, Gresley produced a very large 0-6-0 type with 4ft 8in diameter wheels, and a boiler of new design, with a working pressure of 180lb per sq in. Darlington produced the engines, and when new they were attached to new 'Group Standard' 4,200 gallon tenders; later in 1932-4 these were replaced by smaller 3,500 gallon standard tenders, and the larger ones transferred to new engines of Classes J39, D49 and 02.

The engines proved most satisfactory, but Gresley realised that a larger-wheeled version would be even more versatile and useful, so no further 'J38s' were built, and instead he produced the Class J39 (see Section 13) with 5ft 2in wheels. The 'J38' had a boiler 6in longer and smoke box 6in shorter than the 'J39', but otherwise, apart from the smaller wheels, the two types were basically identical. Many carried 'J39' boilers in later years.

The engines were built as follows:

Nos 1400-1447   Darlington   1926

These later became LNER Nos 5900-5934 respectively, and BR added 60000 to these numbers in 1948.

The class was always associated with the Scottish Area, although the first one was sent to London for inspection by the LNER directors, when new. The 'J38s' were vacuum-fitted, and did some passenger work, but the 'J39s' were always preferred for such duties.

Last of class withdrawn: Nos 65901/29 (1967)
None preserved

The basic dimensions of the class were as follows:

Heating surface, tubes
  Large and small: 1,283.0sq ft
  Firebox: 171.5sq ft
Total (evaporative): 1,454.5sq ft
Superheater: 289.0sq ft
  Combined heating surfaces: 1,743.5sq ft
  Superheater elements: 24
Grate area: 26.0sq ft
Tractive effort (at 85 per cent BP): 28,415lb

Below: Class J38 No 1410, photographed at Dunfermline shed, when still attached to the 4,200gal 'Group Standard' tender without coal rails, and with stepped-out copings. Drive to mechanical lubricator off centre coupled axle. The 'J38s' had two inside cylinders of 20in by 26in, and the boiler design proved to be a most excellent steamer. *T. G. Hepburn*

Above: An excursion working to the Fife Coast is seen passing Inverkeithing, in the charge of Class J38 No 1447. Considerable NER influence can be seen in the outward appearance of the engines. *T. G. Hepburn*

Below: Two of a kind. Class J38s Nos 65930 and 65907 (in background) caught by the camera at Thornton, in BR days. The appearance of the class altered very little over the years except for the substitution of the smaller flush-sided tenders, and the application of BR aws equipment in their final years. *W. J. V. Anderson*

SECTION 13

0-6-0 LNER Class J39, BR Power Class 4F (later 5F)
Goods Engines
Introduced: 1926
Total: 289

The 0-6-0 wheel arrangement was a popular one for over a century of British steam design, and one of the finest examples of the type ever produced was undoubtedly Gresley's Class J39, which was constructed in quantity over the period 1926-1941; to become the most prolific of his locomotive designs in service on the LNER. They were in fact big engines for their kind, and proved to be excellent mixed-traffic performers, able to accelerate rapidly on passenger work, as well as possessing excellent haulage capacity on goods and mineral traffic.

The 'J39' was, as described in the previous section, a larger-wheeled (5ft 2in) version of the 'J38' and the big boiler had a working pressure of 180lb per sq in. As the engines were not intended for long through running, a smaller than usual 24 element superheater was considered sufficient. The cylinders were 20in diameter by 26in stroke.

The engines were built as follows:

Nos 1448-1452/4/5/6 /7/8/9/81/84/92-95	Darlington	1926
Nos 1270, 1496-98, 1233, 1255, 1263, 1259, 1265-67, 1272/3, 1268/9, 1274/77 /75/81/2/6/7/9/90/5/6/8	Darlington	1927
Nos 2691-2730	Darlington	1928/29
Nos 2731-2742	Darlington	1929
Nos 2770-2785, 1418/25	Darlington	1929
Nos 1466/29/70/87/89/91	Darlington	1930
Nos 2786-2788	Darlington	1930
Nos 2962-2970	Darlington	1931
Nos 2971-2976	Darlington	1932
Nos 2977-2980	Darlington	1932
Nos 1453/69/71/80/2/3	Darlington	1932/33
Nos 1412/63/7/8/72	Darlington	1934
Nos 1488/90/75-79	Darlington	1934
Nos 1436/60/4/5/73/4 /85/6 1504-06, 1584	Darlington	1935
Nos 2941-2953, 2981-2994	Darlington	1935
Nos 2995-3000	Darlington	1936
Nos 1803/13/24/8/54/6 /7/69/70, 1532-34/6 /9/40/43-45/7	Beyer, Peacock	1936
Nos 1563/77/80/5-7 1875, 1880, 1894	Beyer, Peacock	1937
Nos 1508/9/35/7/8/41/2 /6/8/51/8/60, 1804/8 1835/62/96/63/98, 1903/22/6/7/8/30/3/ 40/2/3/52/65/71/4/7 80/4/96/7	Darlington	1938
Nos 3081-3098	Darlington	1941

As can be discerned from the above list, the numbering of the class was extremely haphazard, and not even in sequence within each batch built. This was put right by the LNER when, in the sequence shown above, the entire class was renumbered to become Nos 4700-4988. British Railways added 60000 to these numbers.

The tenders attached to the class were, in the main, 'Group Standard' 3,500 gallon type; some flushsided. These were the 'J39/1' variety. 'J39/2' had the larger 4,000 gallon standard tenders. 'J39/3' applied to Nos 4842-45 and Nos 4855-59. The former

Below: The drawing depicts standard Class J39 with large 'Group Standard' tender attached ('J39/2'). Most had the smaller 3,400gal version ('J39/1').

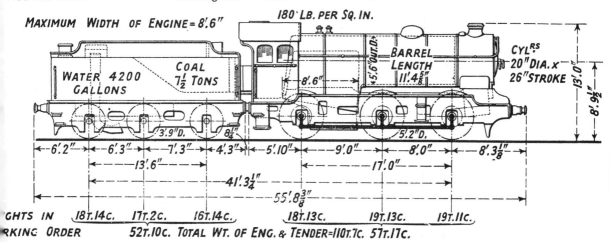

Below: Gresley's standard 0-6-0 Class J39/1, the 'maid of all work' of the LNER from 1926 until the final days of steam, of which no fewer than 289 engines were constructed, in steady numbers each year until 1941, with the exception of 1938/39. No 1269 is seen, on shunting duties, when new, with smaller 'Group Standard' 3,500gal tender attached. Some engines ran with the large 4,200gal version, whilst in 1934 Nos 1475-1479 were delivered to traffic with the secondhand tenders from the Raven Pacifics, which latter engines then received Doncaster pattern tenders instead. *LPC*

Bottom: The later flush sided version of the smaller 3,500gal 'Group Standard' tender is seen here attached to new Class J39/1 No 2726, at the head of a Southend train in 1929. New Gresley Class B17 No 2804 *Elvedon* is seen overtaking with a down Cromer express. No 2726 has both Westinghouse air brakes and the vacuum brake, and has a steam heating hose on the front bufferbeam.
R. Piedot

Left: Class J39/1 0-6-0 No 64725 and Class O2/3 2-8-0 No 63983 come to grips with the 1 in 100 bank between Clipstone West and Welbeck Colliery Junction, at the head of a mineral train from Clipstone Concentration Sidings to Mottram, on 15 April 1950. Both engines are in the early BR black livery, with 'British Railways' painted in full, in Gill Sans, on the tender. *J. Cupit*

Below: A batch of Class J39s delivered as late as 1941 from Darlington utilised some spare tenders from scrapped NER engines of Class D17 and some from Class D21s which were still in service. (These received spare GNR tenders instead). Illustrated is No 64981, originally LNER No 3091, with one of the ex-NER tenders attached; photographed at Gorton in May 1952. These engines were classified as Class J39/3. *Ian Allan Library*

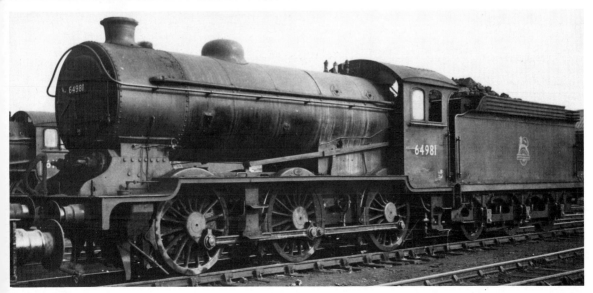

Above: A northbound goods ascending the bank into Wetherby hauled by Class J39/1 0-6-0 No 64863 and Class B16/1 No 61466, in August 1953. Showing location of vacuum chamber on the top of the water tank in the tender. *Cecil G. Pearson*

Right: Class J39/2 No 64948 simmers in the roundhouse at Carlisle Canal shed in April 1957. One of the classic poses available to the camera in the days of steam. *R. E. Vincent*

were attached to NER type 3,940 gallon tenders from scrapped Class B13 engines; the latter had 4,125 gallon tenders which originally belonged to the NER Raven Pacifics (which received Gresley pattern tenders in their place).

These popular and hard-working engines were widely allocated over the system (principally in England), and they underwent very little alteration throughout the lives, so sound and simple was their basic design.

Last of class withdrawn: Nos 64786/90/5, 64822/46/50/75/86 (1962)
None preserved

The basic dimensions of the class were as follows:

Heating surface, tubes
    Large and small: 1,226.28sq ft
    Firebox: 171.5sq ft
Total (evaporative): 1,397.78sq ft
Superheater: 271.8sq ft
    Combined heating surfaces: 1,669.58sq ft
    Superheater elements: 24
Grate area: 26.0sq ft
Tractive effort (at 85 per cent BP): 25,664.0lb

SECTION 14

4-4-0 (3-cyl) LNER Class D49 BR Power Class 4P Passenger Engines
Introduced: 1927
Total: 76

The boiler designed for the Class J39 0-6-0s had proved to be an excellent one in everyday service, and when Gresley turned his attention to a need for some new passenger engines for intermediate duties, he utilised this boiler as the basis for a large three-cylinder 4-4-0 type, thus making them an economical engine to build. It was the first new LNER passenger engine design (the Pacifics dating back to GNR days) and the last new design of the 4-4-0 wheel arrangement to be introduced on that railway. When first placed in service these engines, which were classified 'D49', were the largest 4-4-0s in the British Isles, but some three years later this distinction was lost to the SR Maunsell 'Schools' class.

By using a three-cylinder layout, Gresley thus commenced application of this feature to locomotives other than the principal heavy duty types, a trend that was later even extended to include some new tank engines. One difference apparent in the new Class D49 4-4-0s was the layout of the two-to-one rocking levers to the valve spindle of the inside cylinder; these were placed behind the cylinders (which were all in line) instead of in front of them. This was made possible because the drive from all three cylinders was on to the front coupled axle.

Some stylistic features of the Class D49 4-4-0s echoed Darlington practice, rather than Doncaster. In particular there was the smokebox door and cab style, and the earlier engines had the first Darlington-designed 4,200 gallon 'Group Standard' tenders, with stepped-out sides. Nonetheless the overall appearance was Gresley inspired and had a pleasantly balanced modern air about it, in particular the characteristically delicate motion parts. One curious feature was the rectangular box located on the running plates just ahead of the leading splasher, on Class D49/1 engines. This housed the top of the expansion link in the outside Walschaerts valve motion. Livery when new was full LNER apple green passenger livery.

Gresley's constant interest in valve gear design found further expression in the 'D49s'. There were first of all the three-cylinder conjugated Walschaerts engines, 'D49/1', with piston valves, of which 20 were built in 1927/28 (and a further eight in 1929). Then there were six built in 1928 with Walschaerts valve gear with poppet valves, using oscillating-cam operated valves; these were classified 'D49/3'. These six engines were later rebuilt to conform to Class D49/1. The remaining 48 engines of the total of 76 in the class were delivered with rotary cam poppet valve gear and constituted the 'D49/2s' and the 'D49/4s', which after some modification to their forward gear all became 'D49/2s'.

The engines were built as follows:

Nos 234/51/53/56/64-66 /36/70/77/45/81/46/49 /50, 306/7/9-11	Darlington	1927/28
Nos 318/20/22/27/35/29*	Darlington	1928

*Indicates fitted with Walschaerts valve gear and oscillating cam poppet valves (D49/3), when new, later removed.

Below: The drawing depicts the Class D49/1, with Walschaerts valve gear.

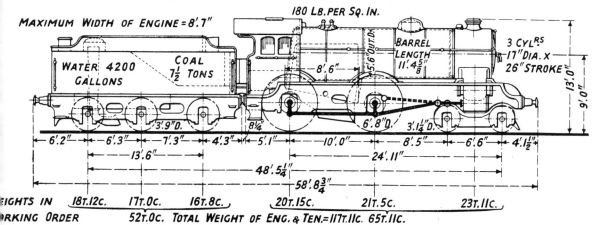

Above: Class D49/1 4-4-0 No 234 *Yorkshire,* the first engine delivered from Darlington, in October 1927. Seen here at the head of a Newcastle-Liverpool express at Wormald Junction. Fitted with the Westinghouse brake to operate the brakes on the engine and tender, this was later replaced by steam brakes. Steam reverse was fitted when new, but this was later replaced by the screw reverse. Other features to note are the small casing around the base of the safety valves, and the rectangular box on the running plate, which housed the top of the expansion link in the outside Walschaerts valve motion. *A. P. Reavil*

Below: The Class D49s were always associated with the North East of England and with Scotland throughout their careers. One engine was however allocated to Kings Cross for a while in 1929. This was No 245 *Lincolnshire,* seen here on shed in positively sparkling condition. While at Kings Cross the engine was handled by Driver William Sparshatt who produced some excellent performances with her on the GN main-line, including the 'Leeds Pullman' and 'Queen of Scots Pullman' workings. Fitted with the first version of the 'Group Standard' 4,200gal tender, with stepped-out coping. *LPC*

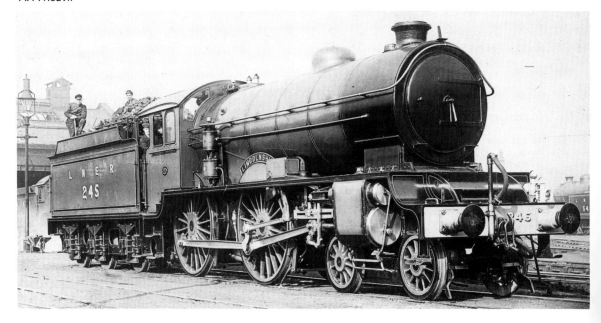

Nos 352/36†	Darlington	1929
Nos 2753-2760	Darlington	1929
Nos 201/11/20/32/35/47/ 55/69/73/82†	Darlington	1932
Nos 283/88/92/97/98†	Darlington	1933
Nos 205/14/17/22/26/30 /38/58/74/79†	Darlington	1934
Nos 353/57/59/61/62†	Darlington	1934
Nos 363-66/68/70/74 /75-77†	Darlington	1934/35

The haphazard numbering at first used was replaced in 1946 by the series Nos 2700-2775, in the order of building shown above. BR added 60000 to these numbers in 1948. All the engines received the names of counties (mostly 'Shires'), and Hunts. In later days all the 'Counties' (or 'Shires') were Class D49/1 and all the 'Hunts' were Class D49/2, more by coincidence than intent. It will be noted that the Nos 2753-2760 were used twice. The easiest way to distinguish these individual engines in photographs is by means of the fact that the original Nos 2753-2760 (which became Nos 2728-2735 in 1946) were 'Shires', whilst the second Nos 2753-2760 were 'Hunts'.

When the first engine, No 234, appeared it was nameless, but soon became *Yorkshire*. Five other engines of the first batch received the names of English counties, and were allocated to Neville Hill shed, Leeds. The other 14 engines were given the names of Scottish counties and went to Scottish Area sheds. Generally speaking the Scottish engines were given harder work to do, right through

†Indicates fitted with Lentz rotary cam poppet valves (D49/2 and D49/4; later all D49/2).

their lives. They were not all that popular with the enginemen, in particular because they proved to be very rough riding, and could throw the poor fireman about, causing bruising. Nevertheless they proved competent engines and, rough riding apart, they were spoken well of for their abilities when deputising for heavier power.

The 'D49/3' engines with Walschaerts valve gear and oscillating-cam Lentz poppet valves, were troublesome and underwent some modification, but still did not prove a great success, and Gresley had these rebuilt with ordinary piston valves in 1938 when the cylinders became due for renewal. These engines had one distinctive feature when new, in the form of outside steampipes to the cylinders, but these were removed on rebuilding.

The 'D49/4' engines had seven different cam positions for forward gear, compared with five positions on the 'D49/2's, and the latter engines were modified to match; all then becoming 'D49/2' and the classification 'D49/4' becoming vacant. In 1942 Edward Thompson rebuilt No 365 *The Morpeth* as an inside two-cylinder engine; this Class D49/2 rebuilt will be described in greater detail in Appendix 2 of this work.

Below: Gresley's interest in valve gear design led him to build six 'Shires' with Walschaerts valve gear and oscillating-cam Lentz poppet valves. These engines, otherwise basically similar to the 'D49/1' series, were classified 'D49/3', and were the first to receive outside steampipes to the cylinders. No casing around base of the safety valves, and screw reverse, with arm curved at both ends. One of this series, No 335 *Bedfordshire,* ran with an MLS multiple valve regulator in the smokebox. Illustrated here is No 327 *Nottinghamshire.* All were converted to 'D49/1' series in 1938, losing their outside steampipes. *LPC*

Below: In 1929 two engines were delivered to traffic fitted with Lentz rotary-cam poppet valve gear, and named after 'Shires'. The second one, No 336 *Buckinghamshire,* is seen here in new condition, with Westinghouse air pump fitted. *LPC*

Bottom: Class D49/1 No 2755 *Berkshire,* built in 1929, and attached to the later flush-sided version of the 4,200gal 'Group Standard' tender. Screw reverse fitted. No 2755 was renumbered 2370 in the 1946 scheme, and the second No 2755 was originally No 226 *The Bilsdale. LPC*

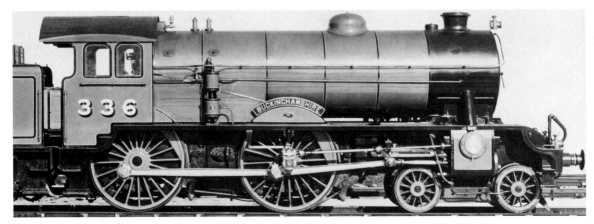

In BR days a further valve gear experiment was carried out on No 62764 *The Garth.* This came about because just as World War 2 broke out Gresley had fitted No 365 *The Morpeth* with an infinitely-variable rotary cam poppet valve gear, with the valves controlled by steam pressure instead of springs. This gear caused trouble in service and when the engine had to visit the works in 1941 for repairs to the camshaft, this was removed, and eventually No 365 emerged as Thompson's two-cylinder rebuild, mentioned above. The removed gear was stored throughout the war and then in 1949 it was replaced by BR on No 62764; with a change to spring-controlled valves. Known as the Reidinger RR type, this gear was put to the test at Rugby Testing Station and then in everyday service, remaining on No 62764 until withdrawal.

Tender types varied with the batches, with the first 28 engines having the first type of 4,200 gallon 'Group Standard' tender. Later some had the flush-sided version, and some received second-hand 4,200 gallon tenders from Class J38 0-6-0s (which in turn received new 3,500 gallon tenders). The final 25 'D49s' built had the large flush-sided 'Group Standard' tenders, with vacuum brakes, for which the cylinder was mounted on the tank top. In the course of time some 'Group Standard' tenders were taken for use on other classes, mainly the 'V2' 2-6-2s, and 'O2' 2-8-0s, and the engines concerned received secondhand ex-NER 4,125 gallon or ex-GCR 4,000 gallon tenders. In the period 1948-50 Darlington rebuilt 10 of the ex-GCR tenders by fitting new flush-sided tanks and bunkers to the existing frames and wheels.

Designed essentially for intermediate passenger duties, the 'D49s' were in their heyday in prewar times. The very heavy loads of the 1941-45 era did not really suit them, and in the North East area

Above: A further 15 engines fitted with Lentz rotary cam poppet valve gear were built in 1932/33. Illustrated is No 211 *The York and Ainsty* (all 15 were named after Hunts), standing at York. The nameplates on these 'Hunt' Class D49s had a cast of a fox above the name; the fox facing forwards on both sides of the engine. Drainpipes from cylinder cocks lengthened towards front of engine. *Real Photographs Co.*

Below: Late in 1939, No 365 *The Morpeth* was fitted with infinitely-variable rotary cam poppet valve gear, with steam-operated valves. Operation of this in traffic proved troublesome, and the gear was removed from No 365 early in 1941. Wartime conditions were hardly the best suited to conduct such experiments! The engine was subsequently rebuilt by Edward Thompson as a two-cylinder, inside cylinder 4-4-0 (see p.160). No 365 is seen when just fitted with the gear, and attached to a flush-sided vacuum-braked 4,200gal tender, with the vacuum cylinder just visible on the rear of the tender tank top. The valve gear was stored, and refitted to No 62764 *The Garth,* in 1949 (see later). *National Railway Museum*

double-heading was sometimes resorted to. The postwar days witnessed the steady introduction of more and more examples of Thompson's versatile two-cylinder Class B1 4-6-0 mixed-traffic engines, and these gradually ousted the 'D49s' from some of their characteristic duties. The advent of the BR diesel railcars, and then the diesel locomotives, finally sounded their death knell, and withdrawals began in 1957.

Last of class withdrawn: Nos 62711/29 (1961)
Example preserved: LNER No 246 *Morayshire*

One withdrawn engine, No 62712, actually survived intact for longer, serving until January 1962 as a stationary boiler to supply steam to an Edinburgh laundry. This was the locomotive which was subsequently privately purchased for preservation and restoration, to become LNER No 246 *Morayshire*.

The basic dimensions of the class were as follows:

Heating surface, tubes
Large and small: 1,226.28sq ft
Firebox: 171.5sq ft
Total (evaporative): 1,397.78sq ft
Superheater: 271.8sq ft
Combined heating surfaces: 1,669.58sq ft
Superheater elements: 24
Grate area: 26.0sq ft
Tractive effort (at 85 per cent BP): 21,556.0sq ft

Class D49/2 No 62773 *The South Durham* makes a fine study at the head of an express leaving Leeds. British Railways dressed the 'D49s' in their mixed-traffic black livery, with LNWR-style lining out. No 62773 looks quite spick and span in these colours, with the original large Lion & Wheel totem on the tender. *Eric Treacy*

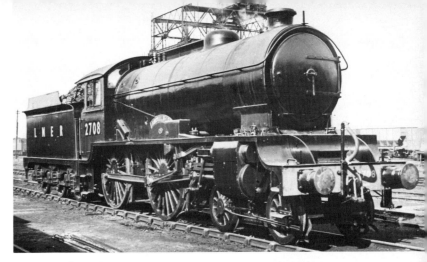

Top right: In plain postwar black LNER livery, with unshaded Gill sans numerals and lettering, Class D49/1 No 2708 *Argyllshire* is seen fresh from overhaul at Darlington in August 1947, with an ex-GCR 4,000gal tender attached. No Class D49 engine received the postwar LNER green livery, and in BR days they were not considered candidates for the Brunswick green, which would probably have suited them quite well. *Photomatic*

Centre right: A further valve gear experiment took place in 1949, when No 62764 *The Garth* was selected by BR for trials fitted with the Reidinger type RR infinitely-variable rotary valve gear that had been removed from No 365, *The Morpeth,* by Edward Thompson in 1941. The engine was sent to the Rugby testing station for trials, as seen here, and then entered service with the gear fitted, in the North Eastern area. It ran with this gear for the remainder of its life. *B. W. Anwell*

Below: Class D49/1 No 62717 *Banffshire* photographed in ex-Works condition at Darlington in May 1958; finished in BR mixed-traffic black livery. The engine has an ex-NER tender attached, which it received in 1953; having previously ran with an ex-GCR tender attached since 1941. *K. R. Pirt*

4-6-2 (3-cyl) LNER Class A3, BR Power Class 7P Express Passenger Engines
Introduced: 1927
Total: 78*

The emergence from Doncaster with a new 220lb per sq in boiler of Class A1 Pacific engine No 4480 *Enterprise* in July 1927, marked the beginning of the development of the Class A3 Pacifics. This move was initially undertaken as an experiment, when further spare boilers were required for the Class A1 Pacifics, and Gresley decided to meet this need by constructing some boilers with higher pressure, for comparative purposes. The new boiler was of improved design and construction and featured a 43-element superheater. Total weight of the locomotive, fitted with the boiler, was increased by 3.8 tons.

The second engine to be given a 220lb per sq in boiler was No 2544 *Lemberg,* and this had the cylinders lined up to 18¼in, whereas No 4480, and the three that followed it, Nos 2573/8/80, retained their 20in cylinders. So all the lessons of the 1925 exchange trials were now put to the practical test, with one important difference, and that was the use by Gresley of a large superheater.

The decision was taken to convert all the existing 'A1's to high-pressure 'A3's as they became due for boiler renewals, and that all new construction would have the 220lb boiler. The 'A3's were sometimes referred to as 'Super Pacifics', to distinguish them from the 'A1's.

New construction, between August 1928 and February 1935, accounted for a further 27 engines,

*Total includes 51 rebuilt from Classes A1 and A10.

Below: Class A3 Pacific, with later style flush-sided non-corridor tender and 'banjo dome' on the boiler.

and these had the long-travel valves and valve gear arrangement produced by Spencer after the 1925 trials. The maximum cut-off remained set at 65 per cent. Detail differences included the provision of new type high-sided non-corridor tenders for some engines, and the fitting of 'banjo domes' to the final batch of nine engines, Nos 2500-8. This distinctive banjo-shaped dome cover housed a slotted steam collector, instead of the usual dome arrangement, in which the steam passed through a series of transverse slots in the top of the boiler barrel before reaching the regulator valve. This was to prevent priming, as any excessive moisture was held by the slots, and allowed to fall back into the boiler barrel. Another change resulted from the decision to standardise on left-hand drive; earlier engines being altered to this layout in BR days. The reboilering of the 'A1's was interrupted by the Second World War, and it was not until December 1948 that the last conversion to Class A3 took place; this was BR No 60068 *Sir Visto.* Following experience with the first five engines all the new construction of 'A3's, and the subsequent conversions from 'A1's, were given cylinders of 19in diameter; the first five conversions were duly brought into line.

Some enginemen voiced complaints to Nigel Gresley because they were worried that their view of the road ahead was on occasions being obscured by drifting smoke and steam on the 'A3's. This was a known problem with a number of large-boilered types with small chimneys, and indeed had been established as the cause of an accident with a 'Royal Scot' class 4-6-0 on the LMSR. With the 'A3's the trouble mainly arose when the engines were running in early cut-off, and it was distinctly a feature that arose after the fitting of the long-travel valves. To improve their smoke lifting in these running conditions, Gresley undertook a number of experiments on two 'A3's, Nos 2747 *Coronach* and 2751 *Humorist.* A further experiment took place in 1937 when *Humorist* was again selected, and fitted with a double-chimney and Kylchap blastpipe. It ran throughout the war years in this condition, and

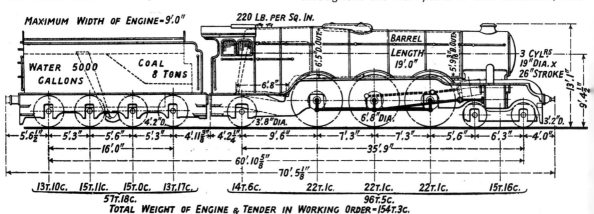

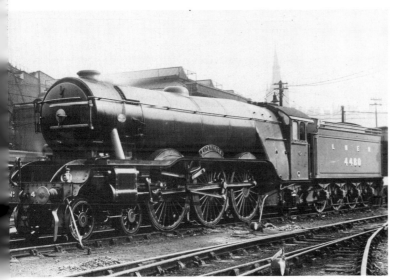

Above: Class A1 Pacific No 4480 rebuilt with the first 220lb per sq in boiler and Robinson 43-element superheater, and reclassified 'A3' (Class A2 was occupied by the Raven Pacifics of the former NER). The new boilers were easily identified by the square cover plates on the upper sides of the smokebox, which housed the outer ends of the enlarged superheater. In this picture No 4480 *Enterprise* retains the large chimney, dome and the high cab of the GNR loading gauge. *LPC*

Centre left: In this later view of No 4480 *Enterprise,* the 'A3' type 220lb boiler has received the smaller chimney and dome, and the cab roof has been modified in order to suit it for running over the Scottish lines. *Enterprise* retained its cylinders of 20in diameter when first reboilered. The second engine, No 2544 *Lemberg,* had the cylinders lined up to 18¼in. The three other new boilers were fitted to Nos 2573/78/80, and these also retained their 20in cylinders. *LPC*

Bottom left: Class A3 Pacific No 2580 *Shotover,* with one of the corridor tenders attached, for the London-Edinburgh non-stops. A Pullman-type gangway and buckeye coupling ensured a good connection between the tender and the leading carriage. Note the porthole window, to illuminate the interior of the gangway, running down the right hand side of the tender. *LPC*

Right: Production version of the Class A3 Pacific, No 2750 *Papyrus* on the turntable at Kings Cross, and carrying the 'Flying Scotsman' headboard. The engine has one of the corridor tenders attached. No 2750 was the last 'A3' to run with one of these tenders (until September 1937), once the LNER decided to transfer the corridor tenders to their new Class A4 streamlined Pacifics (see p122). The following Class A3 Pacifics ran with corridor tenders at some time: Nos 2506/8/73/80, 2743-6/9/50/2/95/6. Not all were used on the non-stop workings, however. *LPC*

gained a reputation for good steaming and free running.

The new engines of the class were built as follows:

Nos 2743-2752	Doncaster	1928/29
Nos 2595-2599	Doncaster	1930
2795-2797		
Nos 2500-2508	Doncaster	1934/35

In 1946 No 2598 was renumbered No 565, No 2500 was 570 and No 2505 was 575 for a short period, then all the production 'A3s' were renumbered as follows (new numbers shown in brackets): Nos 2743-2752 (Nos 89-98), Nos 2595-2599 (Nos 84-88), Nos 2795-2797 (Nos 99-101) and Nos 2500-2508 (Nos 35-43). BR added 60000 to these numbers in 1948.

So much has been published on the performances of the Class A3 Pacifics that it would be pointless to repeat it in any great detail here. In

Above: No 2743 *Felstead* was the first of a new batch of Pacifics, and went into service in August 1928. These new 'A3s' had 19in cylinder diameter, and the earlier conversions were altered to match. Twenty-seven engines were built between 1928-37. Originally paired with a corridor tender, *Felstead* is seen here with a non-corridor tender of GNR type. Left-hand drive was standard for the production 'A3s'. Photographed on an up express near Hatfield, in 1937. *Photomatic*

prewar days they were kept in fine fettle, and produced some noble exploits as well as maintaining very good everyday running. Even the coming of the streamlined 'A4' Pacifics did not affect their reputation, and they continued to be the mainstay of East Coast main line express passenger traffic, although they lost their corridor tenders to the 'A4's which took over the non-stop workings. To an 'A3' No 4472, went the accolade of the first really reliably recorded 100mph running, and during the test runs of No 2750 *Papyrus,* with 217 tons gross, in March

Above: Class A3 No 2580 *Shotover* was fitted with an ACFI feedwater pump in 1929 (at the same time an A1, No 2576 *The White Knight,* also received one). The heater was placed in the front of the smokebox, ahead of the chimney. These two engines ran in this form for several years. *Collection: A. Swain*

Centre left: Problems of drifting smoke, causing lack of vision from the footplate, had been highlighted by an accident at Leighton Buzzard on the LMSR in 1931, when the driver of a 'Royal Scot' class 4-6-0 had been unable to see the road ahead. This was a troublesome feature of large-boilered engines with small chimneys, and Gresley decided to try out some experiments to improve smoke-lifting on his Pacifics. First of Class A3 No 2747 *Coronach* was modified at Doncaster in October 1931, with the upper part of the smokebox partitioned off to make an air duct with a vent behind the chimney. A similar arrangement was then applied to No 2751 *Humorist,* except that a dual chimney was fitted, with the air leaving via the rear of the two chimneys. No 2751 is seen in this form on a down express at Harringay in July 1932. Note anti vacuum valve on superheater header casing. *Photomatic*

Bottom left: After some further experiments with a single semi-annular pattern chimney, without much success, *Humorist* was again altered in March 1933 by Doncaster, so that the top of the smokebox was cut away around the base of the single stovepipe chimney, and two small wind vanes were fitted. This beautiful study of the engine somehow emphasises the flowing lines of the front end and running plate which were a hallmark of these classic Pacifics. Anti-vacuum valve still located on the superheater header casing. *British Rail ER*

1935, the engine ran at an average of 100.6mph for the 12.3 miles from Corby to Tallington; making the London-Newcastle round trip of 536.6 miles in 468 minutes 55 seconds.

During World War 2, when the grand episode of high speed running gave way to one of enormous loads (sometimes more than 20 carriages and over 700 tons), and of indifferent maintenance, the Gresley 'A3s' began to suffer badly although they still performed prodigiously. The conjugated valve gear was more affected by lack of attention than the valve gear on two-cylinder engines, and this could be described as their Achilles Heel. Even the initial postwar period saw little immediate improvement, and to make matters worse there was poor quality coal to cope with, and a chronic shortage of enginemen; with the result that these splendid machines were left to suffer at the hands of men lacking in expertise. By the mid 1950s one could

have been forgiven for thinking that the Class A3 Pacifics had definitely had their day; events however were to prove otherwise!

In retrospect it seems odd that it should have taken nearly 20 years for the lessons learned with No 2751 *Humorist,* the Kylchap engine, to be applied to the rest of the class. But this was so, and although the enginemen knew *Humorist* to be an excellent runner and free steamer, it was not until 1957 that BR applied the Kylchap double blastpipe to the rest of the class. The results were remarkable, and allied to some improvements to the design of the valve gear which were undertaken by Mr K. J. Cook (who moved from Swindon to Doncaster to become Chief Mechanical & Electrical Engineer there), the 'A3's were suddenly given a wonderful new lease of life. One interesting alteration was the increase of the maximum cut-off from 65 to 75 per cent. Anyone who travelled behind a Kylchap-fitted 'A3' in the

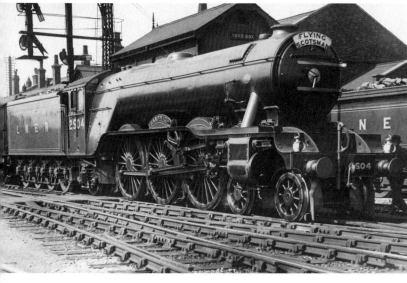

Above left: Class A3 Pacific No 2504 *Sandwich* standing at Grantham with the up 'Flying Scotsman'; with left hand drive and new type non-corridor tender. The 1934 building programme of nine Class A3 Pacifics was the final batch ordered, and Nos 2500-8 were all given the new type tenders. Another variation was the 'banjo dome' on the boiler, which housed a slotted steam collector instead of the usual dome arrangement.
T. G. Hepburn

Left: Working a down slow train, No 2507 *Singapore* was caught by the camera at Peterborough about 1936. The design of the water column in the lefthand background is noteworthy! No 2507 shows the location of the reversing lever on the left-hand drive engines. Banjo dome on boiler, and new type non-corridor tender attached. *T. G. Hepburn*

Above: Humorist again; this time fitted with a Kylchap double blastpipe and chimney. The softer exhaust led to complaints from enginemen that their vision was obscured by drifting smoke; but the engine gained a good reputation for steaming and free-running. No 2751 is seen here at Barkston , running-in on a Doncaster-Peterborough slow train in 1937, when just fitted with the Kylchap exhaust. *T. G. Hepburn*

Centre left: By the time this picture of *Humorist* was taken, in wartime black livery with the initials NE on the tender, but renumbered with the new postwar No 97, the engine had undergone yet another change to the chimney and smoke deflecting layout, although the Kylchap exhaust was retained. The engine was photographed at Grantham, and shows front footsteps added. *T. G. Hepburn*

Bottom left: Close-up of the GNR type tender on No 77 *The White Knight,* showing style of lining-out used for the rear panel. In postwar LNER apple green livery, with shaded letters and numerals, the engine was photographed at Grantham in July 1948, still retaining right hand drive. *H. C. Casserley*

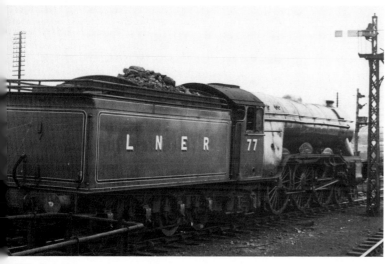

Left: After an experiment with ultramarine blue and LNW type lining, a lighter shade, similar to Caledonian blue, was selected by BR for its principal express passenger locomotives, with black and white lining and a large Lion and Wheel totem on the tender. This was the standard livery for the 'A3s' from May 1949 to August 1951 when it was abandoned because it did not wear well, and replaced by Brunswick green. No 60064 *Tagalie* is seen in the blue livery, leaving Stoke Tunnel on an up Bradford express, in June 1951. *J. P. Wilson*

Below: In very grubby blue livery No 60097 *Humorist* displays yet another change to its smoke deflecting arrangements, with full-size deflectors alongside the smokebox, but retaining the stovepipe double chimney. Photographed on an up express at Dalton Bank, in May 1950, with the majority of the rolling stock still in LNER mock-teak livery. *Photomatic*

later part of the 1950s or early 1960s, will recall the excellent condition they were kept in and the fine running they were then achieving; often showing a clean pair of heels to the new diesel locomotives that were supposed to replace them!

One strange oversight was the lack of provision of smoke deflectors for the Kylchap 'A3's when first converted – despite all the experience that had been gained with *Humorist* over the years. The final form arrived at, based upon German practice, was extremely effective and incidentally gave a more modern and arrogant look to Gresley's thoroughbreds, some of which were approaching 40 years of age.

Whole books have been devoted to the story of these classic machines and the reader in search of greater detail is commended to them, for the saga of the Gresley 'A1's and 'A3's is truly remarkable. Even

today, with the legendary No 4472 *Flying Scotsman* still in steam, the story is not over by any means.

Last of class withdrawn: 60052 (1966)
Example preserved: BR No 60103 (LNER 4472)

The basic dimensions of the class, in LNER production series form (mid-1930s) were as follows:

Heating surface, tubes
  Large and small: 2,476.8sq ft
  Firebox: 215.0sq ft
Total (evaporative): 2,691.8sq ft
Superheater: 635.5sq ft
  Combined heating surfaces: 3,327.3sq ft
  Superheater elements: 43
Grate area: 41.25sq ft
Tractive effort (at 85 per cent BP): 32,909lb

Above: Class A3 Pacific No 60097 *Humorist* with a new lipped double-chimney casing for its Kylchap exhaust, and repainted in the BR Brunswick green livery seen at the head of the 'Waverley' (St Pancras-Edinburgh) express taking the Waverley route north of Carlisle. New standard BR coaches, with carmine and cream livery, form the train. *Eric Treacy*

Below: In May 1958 it was decided to fit all the Class A3 Pacifics with double chimneys, and this work was completed by January 1960. These double chimneys and blastpipes gave the class a new lease of life, and produced a noticeable improvement in their day-to-day performance. As in the case of *Humorist* in prewar days, however, there were soon complaints of exhaust drifting across the drivers' vision, in cross winds. No 60082 *Neil Gow* was photographed at Leeds Holbeck, waiting to work the down 'Waverley'. *G. W. Morrison*

Top: The first attempt to improve smoke deflection on the double-chimney 'A3s' was similar to that earlier applied to *Humorist,* and consisted of two small vanes alongside the chimney, as seen here on No 60061 *Pretty Polly,* at Kings Cross. Note the vacuum gauge fitted to the side of the smokebox, and shield for BR aws gear behind screw coupling. *P. Ransome-Wallis*

Above: The small wing-type smoke deflectors did not prove very effective, and in 1960 trough type smoke deflectors of German pattern were fitted to four 'A3s' as an experiment (at the suggestion of Mr P. N. Townend, then Shedmaster at Kings Cross). This first appeared on No 60049 *Galtee Moor,* and was so successful that it was applied to the 'A3s' in general, and in due course 55 engines received them. No 60040 *Cameronian* is seen throwing its exhaust high at the head of the 4.15pm freight to Millerhill, leaving Carlisle in April 1964. *S. C. Crook*

Class A3 Pacific No 60051 *Blink Bonny* in fine form at the head of 'The South Yorkshireman Railtour No 2,' in 1964, seen climbing out of Sheffield through Heeley. This gives a splendid picture of how the 'A3s' looked in their last years in BR service, when they were excellent performers. The German smoke deflectors gave them quite a rakish new look. The engine is fitted with BR aws gear below the bufferbeam, and has been converted to left-hand drive. A speedometer is driven from the rear coupled wheels. *K. R. Pirt*

Left: When Class A3 Pacific No 60103 *Flying Scotsman* was purchased for preservation by Mr Alan Pegler, following its withdrawal in January 1963, the trough type smoke deflectors were removed, and a single chimney restored. With these modifications, but still in BR livery, No 60103 is seen running trials between Peterborough and Doncaster, at Essendine in February 1963. The subsequent history of this, and other preserved Gresley engines, is dealt with later. *P. H. Wells*

Bottom left: The last three Class A3s to survive in service (Nos 60051/52/100) received a broad yellow diagonal stripe on the cabsides. This was to denote that they were prohibited from working south of Crewe under the electric catenary (despite the fact that they were then allocated to Edinburgh!). No 60052 *Prince Palatine* is seen running light engine, passing Lochmuir signalbox, Fife, in March 1965, bound for Darlington Works. The engine was in such appalling condition that it was not expected to return, but it did, and ran until January 1966, being the last to be withdrawn. *W. J. V. Anderson*

SECTION 16

4-6-0 (3-cyl) LNER Class B17, BR Power Class 4P (later 5P for B17/6)
Passenger Engines
Introduced: 1928
Total: 73

The Great Eastern Section was feeling the need for a more powerful type of locomotive for all its main lines by late 1926, and indeed so urgent was this becoming that it seems, for once, Gresley was caught unprepared. His drawing office and workshop capacity was already heavily committed, but he nonetheless requested some first studies for the new engine from Doncaster, after Kings Cross had produced a broad outline of what was required. The GE Section had some stringent Civil Engineering restrictions, and this first specification was for a three-cylinder 4-6-0 type with a maximum axle load of only 17 tons. The grate area was to be 30sq ft and the arrangement of the cylinders and motion was to follow the layout he had introduced with his Class D49 4-4-0s, with the two-to-one levers behind the cylinders. It seems that Doncaster had quite a struggle trying to draw up an acceptable locomotive to this lightweight specification; with various attempts being rejected.

Meanwhile the need for new locomotives had become a matter of real urgency, and the outcome of various internal meetings was a decision to place the detailed design work, and the construction, of 20 new 4-6-0s with an outside manufacturer, before Doncaster had produced a successful solution. The North British Locomotive Company was therefore approached to see if it would be prepared to undertake the work of designing and building the required engines. This they agreed to in December 1927. North British had built engines to Gresley's design before (the 'O2's and 'A1's) and held various

detail drawings including those for the 'K3' 2-6-0. For certain items, such as the tender (which had to be of short wheelbase to suit the GE lines) NBL approached Stratford and Darlington; the latter for bogie details.

Even the large drawing office staff and the renowned expertise of NBL seems to have found the specification too exacting, and both the initial schemes submitted to the LNER in February 1928 were for engines of higher axle load than the 17 tons specified (being 18 and 19 tons), whilst the idea of using the Class D49 valve gear arrangement was replaced by the 'A1' Pacific layout. The grate area was smaller than had been requested initially.

The 18-ton axle load proposed was perforce accepted in principle by the LNER, which was therefore obliged to modify the route availability of the proposed new engines from 'all' GE Section lines to 'certain' GE main lines. The initial order of Febrary 1928 was reduced to 10 locomotives, for delivery within a period of from six to ten months. As stated, the NBL possessed a quantity of detail drawings of Gresley origin, and many features of the new 4-6-0s were extracted from these, and in particular from the Class A1 Pacifics. Nevertheless the LNER requested some modifications once the drawings were presented, including an increase in the cylinder diameter and the grate area, and lighter springing. The most significant request was that the conjugated valve gear levers should be located *behind* the cylinders. Here NBL encountered problems, and delays began to build up whilst the drawing office revised the valve gear layout. They could not arrange for all three cylinders to drive on to the middle coupled axle, and as a result the layout

Below: The drawing depicts one of the later engines Nos 2848-2872 ('Football' series) with larger 4,200gal 'Group Standard' tender.

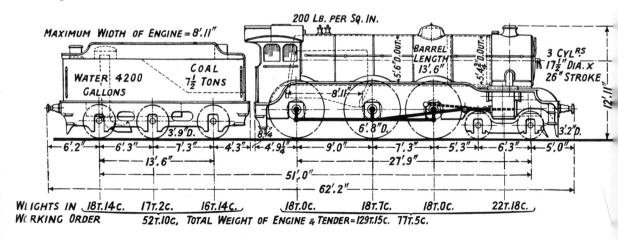

was different from all other Gresley three-cylinder types, the drive being divided. The two outside cylinders drove on to the middle pair of coupled wheels and the inside cylinder, which was located well forward in the frames, drove on to the leading pair. A similar arrangement had been produced for the LMSR Fowler 'Royal Scot' class, introduced in 1927 and also built by NBL. In order to meet the GE Section axleloads the boilers of the Class B17 – as it became known – had to be of light construction; a feature that was to create problems of maintenance throughout their lives. Other problems which were inherent in the original lightweight specification included frame fractures, and somewhat unsatisfactory springing. These led to modifications which, together with variations in the brake systems, created the sub-classifications 'B17/1' – 'B17/4'.

The locomotive numbers in the sub-categories of the Class B17 4-6-0s when built were as follows:

B17/1 Nos 2800-2809
B17/2 Nos 2810-2842
B17/3 Nos 2843-2847
B17/4 Nos 2848-2872

The 'B17/4' series was built for use on other Southern Area lines, and therefore did not have to comply with the severe length restrictions of the GE Section. This meant that they could be fitted with the longer wheelbase 'Group Standard' tender.

The first tender design for the 'B17's was closely based upon GER practice, of 3,700 gallon capacity and mounted on a short wheelbase. The first 15, attached to Nos 2800-15, had Westinghouse brakes;

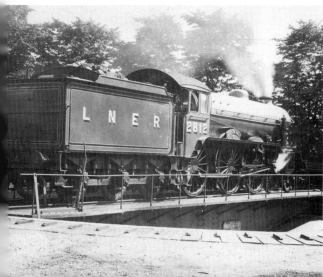

Above: The second engine to be delivered from the North British Locomotive Co. in 1928, is seen here in original form except that the nameplate was at first fitted to the leading splasher. This was quickly moved to the centre splasher by the LNER. Class B17/1 No 2801 *Holkham,* is illustrated. Note the coal piled very high on the short wheelbase tender; this created problems of spillage which were later to be alleviated by adding inner coal guards (see page 98). *A. G. Ellis*

Left: Severe overall length restrictions on the GE Section meant that the 'B17s' had to be paired with new short wheelbase tenders, very similar in design to those coupled to the 'B12' 4-6-0s. No 2812 *Houghton Hall,* fitted with the Westinghouse air brake (note extra hose on tender bufferbeam) illustrates one of these tenders in original form. Locomotive number moved from tender to cabside. *E. R. Wethersett*

97

Nos 2816-42 had steam brakes and Nos 2843-7 were vacuum braked. The tenders for Nos 2848-61 were as just mentioned of the 4,200 gallon 'Group Standard' type, with vacuum brakes.

Although NBL did the design work and the initial construction of the class, for some reason the company did not receive any further orders from the LNER after delivery of the first 10. The engines were built as follows:

Nos 2800-2809	North British	1928
Nos 2810-2821	Darlington	1930
Nos 2822-2836	Darlington	1931
Nos 2837-2842	Darlington	1933
Nos 2843-2847	Darlington	1935
Nos 2848-2861	Darlington	1936
Nos 2862-2872	R. Stephenson & Co.	1937

(The boilers for Nos 2810-2836 were manufactured by Armstrong, Whitworth & Co.)

All the engines were allocated to the Southern Area, and those with GE type tenders were named after English country houses. The final batch, with 'Group Standard' tenders were named after Association Football clubs. A scheme proposed in the late 1930s to build some Class B17s for use in the North East was never carried out, and the new 'V2' class 2-6-2 was substituted.

For publicity purposes two engines of the class, Nos 2859/70, were given 'A4' style streamlining and put to work on the 'East Anglian' between Liverpool Street and Norwich, in September 1937. These became Class B17/5 in this form. It is extremely doubtful whether the streamlining had any practical effect upon the performance of the engines, at the line speeds then permitted on the GE main line.

When Edward Thompson succeeded Gresley as CME he based the boiler design for his highly successful 'B1' class 4-6-0 upon Gresley's 'B17' class boiler, but with the higher working pressure of 225lb

Above: Class B17/2 4-6-0 No 2834 *Hinchinbrooke,* photographed at Nottingham Victoria, shows the higher inner coal guard fitted to some of the shortwheelbase 'B17' tenders. Drainpipes from cylinder cocks lengthened to front of bogie. Steam brakes for engine and tender; vacuum for train. *T. G. Hepburn*

Right: Class B17/2 No 2819 *Welbeck Abbey* leads 14 coaches of GE stock; vacuum fitted. The tender was a makeshift wooden high inner coal guard added. *E. R. Wethersett*

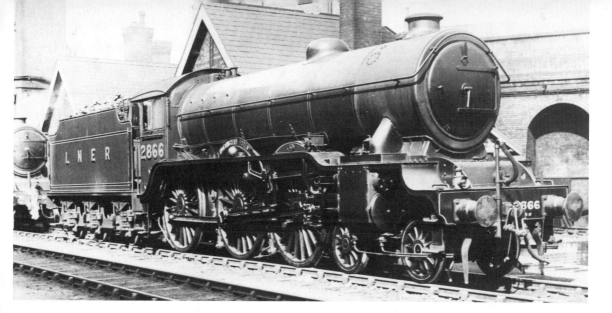

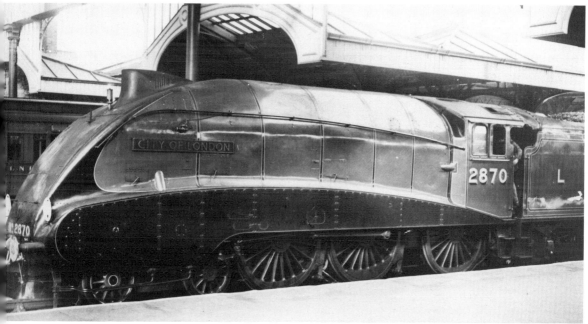

Top: One of the final 'Football' series, of Class B17/4, built by Robert Stephenson & Co. in 1937, and attached to a 4,200gal flush sided 'Group Standard' tender. Photographed awaiting the next spell of duty, at Nottingham Victoria in prewar days. Note the polished brass football below the nameplate, the background colour was the Club's colour, red. *T. G. Hepburn*

Above: The two engines selected for streamlining in 1937 were finished in apple green and black livery, and the coaches of the 'East Anglian' were of standard teak finish, without any streamlining. The 'A4' style front end took up almost a third of the engine's length and made the rear part look very small by comparison. The 4,200gal tenders were modified to look like the larger Pacific streamlined tenders, with built-up side sheets and a rubber sheeting between the cab roof and tender top. No 2870 *City of London* is seen at Norwich Thorpe in May 1939. The two engines retained their casings until 1951, but various pieces were removed during the war to make routine maintenance simpler; in particular the valances that concealed much of the wheels in motion. Plain black livery did little to enhance their form in later years. *J. P. Wilson*

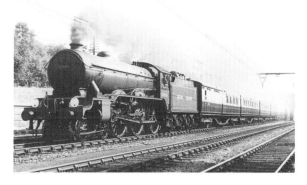

Top: In the plain black livery adopted during wartime, with shaded numerals and lettering, No 1655 *Middlesbrough* was photographed at Stratford in 1947. This engine was one of the eleven vacuum-braked examples of the class that were fitted with Westinghouse brakes during the period February 1940 to April 1942 (Nos 2848/54/5/6/60/1/3/5/8/71/2), when the GE Section was in need of further locomotives so equipped. The brass football was retained on the nameplate splasher but the football club colours were painted out, when the engines were in black livery. *Photomatic*

Above: As part of a nationwide public opinion exercise, in order to find new liveries for the nationalised railways, in the early part of 1948 Class B17 No 61661 *Sheffield Wednesday* was repainted in an experimental bright green. At first, the lining out was yellow, but this was changed to LNWR style red, yellow and grey. It was worked with a set of Gresley stock which was painted in GWR chocolate and cream, to obtain the public's view. No 61665 received a very similar livery, but painted in the true shade of LNER apple green. No 61661 is seen working the repainted stock on a down express near Shenfield in June 1948. *H. C. Casserley*

Left: Rather unnecessarily carrying both an oil lamp and a disc headcode in the same position, Class B17/2 No 61619 *Welbeck Abbey* breezes along in the summer of 1948 with a suburban working, wearing the new BR number 61619 (in modified Gill Sans lettering) on both bufferbeam and cabside, but still painted in the plain black livery. During the war the tenders were lettered NE only.
E. R. Wethersett

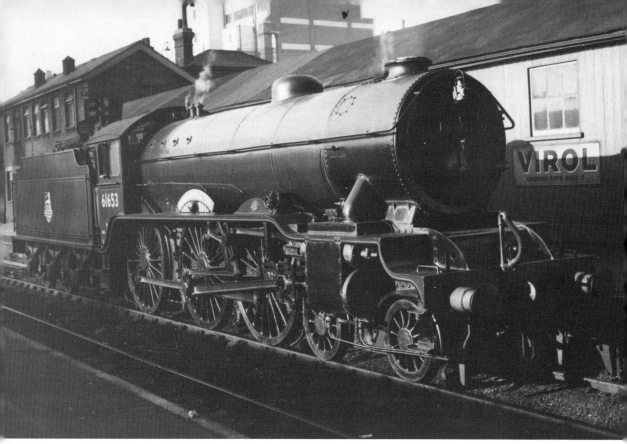

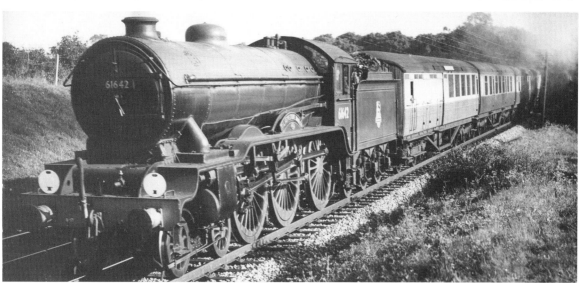

Top: The final livery of the 'B17s', in BR days was dark Brunswick green, with orange and black lining. On the 'Football' series of 'B17s' the club colours were restored to the splashers, below the nameplates, as seen here on No 61653 *Huddersfield Town* (whose colours were blue and white); photographed at Kings Cross. At this time the engine carried an 'A3'-type chimney, which had been fitted at Doncaster by mistake; it was soon removed!

Above: A fine photographic study of a 'B17' in its final days of main line running, before the 'Britannia' Pacifics, and then the Pilot Scheme diesels displaced them. No 61642 *Kilverstone Hall* heads a GE line express, with the coaches painted in the BR carmine red and cream livery in the early 1950s. *Ian Allan Library*

per sq in. In due course some of these boilers were built for use on the 'B17's, and at first this version (as used in 1943) had the pressure reduced to 180lb. Later, between 1947 and 1958, boilers with the higher working pressure were fitted to 55 Class B17s, and these then became Class B17/6.

A more drastic alteration was made to 10 engines of the class, again by Thompson, when they were rebuilt as two-cylinder engines, with the higher pressure boilers. These were reclassified as 'B2' and further details are given in Appendix 2.

Like all Gresley's three-cylinder engines, the 'B17's suffered from the indifferent maintenance standards of World War 2 and its aftermath. A feature which became marked as their mileage between overhauls built up was their tendency to rough ride, and this could become so severe that enginemen were discouraged from any fast running. Generally speaking though, they were hard working engines, and when kept in good fettle, as they were at Ipswich for example, in the 1950s, they could still be made to ride well and run well.

During the periods when first the Standard 'Britannia' Pacifics, and then the Pilot Scheme diesel-electrics, were prone to teething troubles and failures, the 'B17's were quite often called upon to deputise for the new power and to run to the faster timings. That they did so, and upon occasions brilliantly, was a source of much pride to their drivers and shed staff.

Last of class withdrawn: 61668 (1960)
None preserved

The basic dimensions of the class, in prewar LNER standard form were as follows:

Heating surfaces, tubes
  Large and small: 1,508.0sq ft
  Firebox: 168.0sq ft
Total (evaporative): 1,676.0sq ft
Superheater: 344.0sq ft
  Combined heating surfaces: 2,020.0sq ft
  Superheater elements: 24
Grate area: 27.5sq ft
Tractive effort (at 85 per cent BP): 25,380lb

Below: When the two streamlined engines had their casings removed in 1951, they were rebuilt to the Class B17/6 specification with Thompson boilers pressed to 225lb per sq in. At the same time the tenders were destreamlined. No 61670 *City of London* is seen on a train from Yarmouth descending the bank into Liverpool Street, past East London Junction, with an LT electric standing in Shoreditch station in the right background. The dome cover on No 61670 is more angular than the original 'B17' design. *R. E. Vincent*

4-6-4 (4-cyl Compound) LNER Class W1
Express Passenger Engine
Introduced: 1929
Total: 1

Gresley had, by 1929, clearly demonstrated his open minded and forward thinking about valve gears and improved front ends. It was then, perhaps, only a logical further step in his unswerving development of the steam locomotive that he should attempt to introduce a really high pressure boiler for a large and powerful locomotive. In fact he had started to consider such a move as far back as 1924, as a result of studying the impressive design of some contemporary high pressure stationary and marine boilers, with their high overall efficiency. He thought it possible to obtain some similar improvements in efficiency and economy with an adaptation of these high pressure boilers which would be suitable for use on a steam locomotive; although some considerable design problems were involved.

Mr Harold Yarrow was approached by Gresley to see if his Glasgow engineering firm would be prepared to undertake the detail design of a suitable water-tube boiler for a locomotive roughly equivalent in size to the LNER Pacifics. After more than three years of design work an order for one boiler was placed early in 1928. This had a working pressure of 450lb per sq in; considerably higher than normal railway practice. The boiler was patented in the joint names of Gresley and Yarrow.

To carry the boiler, Gresley produced a massive 4-6-4 chassis. Classified W1, the locomotive was given the distinctive numbering 10000. This was built at Darlington works under conditions of some secrecy, and completed in December 1929. Painted in dark battleship grey, the engine had a most unorthodox appearance, with a bulbous casing enclosing the boiler, and with a forward extension of the casing making an aerodynamic screen, which enveloped the chimney and smokebox. Air ducts above the bufferbeam platform, on both sides of the smokebox, led up to the top of the smokebox behind the chimney and were intended to lift the exhaust high over the engine.

To utilise the high pressure steam produced by the boiler, a four cylinder compound front end was designed, with two high pressure cylinders 12in × 26in driving the leading coupled wheels and two low pressure cylinders 20in by 26in driving the centre pair of coupled wheels. (Later the high pressure cylinders were reduced to 10in diameter.) Walschaerts valve gear was fitted, and there were only two outside sets, with the valves of the inside high pressure cylinders operated from the outside gear by rocking shafts.

No 10000 was placed in service on Pacific type duties from Gateshead shed. It was tried out on the 'Flying Scotsman' in the summer of 1930. Gresley very understandably took a close personal interest in the performance of the engine, and he must have been disappointed to discover that it was appreci-

Below: The Class W1 4-6-4 four cylinder compound high pressure locomotive, as first introduced into service; with 5,000gal eight-wheel corridor tender.

Top right: Gresley's 'Hush-Hush' experimental express passenger locomotive (so-called because it was both designed and built with considerable secrecy) is seen here entering Darlington on an up express in June 1930. The large water-tube boiler and its bulbous outer cladding took full advantage of the LNER loading gauge. The boiler bands and handrails were finished in bright burnished steel. The main safety valves, set at 450lb per sq in, one visible on the side of the boiler just behind the handrail. There was also an auxiliary safety valve set at 200lb per sq in on the left hand side of the engine. *Photomatic*

Bottom right: Photographed on a down express near Portobello, in 1930, the impressive bulk of No 10000 here contrasts oddly with the vintage carriage at the head of the train. A popular description of this unconventional locomotive, based upon its appearance, was the monster with wings but no funnel. Not strictly accurate, but the funnel was well hidden! *P. Ransome-Wallis*

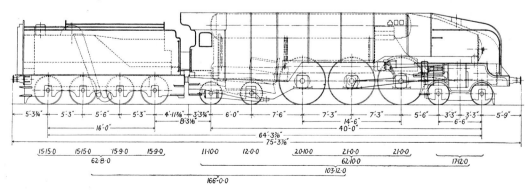

ably heavier on coal than his own Pacifics. There were problems with draughting, and inefficient combustion, and the blastpipe was altered to a double one in an attempt to improve steaming. The boiler walls and the tubes had some slight tendency to leak, resulting in poor steaming. A number of modifications were made to the engine, and in particular to the boiler, and in its final high-pressure form No 10000 ran with a Kylchap double blastpipe. This had a chimney casing similar to that used on the 'A4' Pacifics.

Reluctantly, Gresley eventually decided in 1937 to rebuild No 10000 with a conventional boiler (see Section 22), because the engine did not prove to be economical in everyday service. This bold experiment, typical of both Gresley's and Bulleid's inventive skills, thus came to an end. It should always be remembered however for the considerable design innovation that went into its making. In retrospect the fundamental problem may now be summed-up by comparing the different day-to-day operating conditions experienced by stationary, or marine boilers, as opposed to those which have to ride upon the frames of a constantly vibrating, and swaying, reciprocating steam locomotive. There was also the problem of producing such a boiler within the rigid limitations of the LNER loading gauge, which imposed undesirable restraints upon its internal layout.

Rebuilt 1937 to Class W1 with conventional boiler.

The basic dimensions of the locomotive, as delivered in 1929, were as follows:

Heating surfaces, tubes: 1,067.0sq ft
   Firebox: 919.0sq ft
Total (evaporative): 1,986.0sq ft
Superheater: 140.0sq ft
   Combined heating surfaces: 2,126.0sq ft
Grate area: 34.95sq ft
Tractive effort (at 85 per cent BP): 32,000lb

Below: This most interesting picture was taken on 20 September 1930 at the start of the Railway Centenary celebrations at Liverpool; here the 'Hush-Hush' 4-6-4 is seen in the company the old Liverpool & Manchester Railway engine *Lion.* At this event No 10000 was described as 'the latest and most modern engine in the British Isles'. GWR enthusiasts must have resented this, as their 'King' class 4-6-0 was next to it in line; also LMSR enthusiasts whose 'Royal Scot' and Beyer-Garratt were also there. This view of No 10000, showing the corridor tedner, also emphasises the high pitch of the cab roof and boiler. *Ian Allan Library*

Left: A double blastpipe and additional cowling were applied to No 10000 in efforts to improve steaming and smoke deflection, producing an appearance not dissimilar to that achieved later by Bulleid in his 'Merchant Navy' Pacifics. The engine is seen here in Doncaster works yard. A domeless ex Hull & Barnsley 0-6-0 of LNER Class J23/1 is in the background, with an 0-8-0 beyond.
National Railway Museum

Below: The 4-6-4 (or 'Hudson' to use the American description for its wheel arrangement) is seen here at Newcastle in its final form, whilst still carrying the high pressure boiler. The front end had been modified to give easier access to the smokebox door, and a large Kylchap double blastpipe and chimney were fitted. No 10000 was a somewhat troublesome machine, as might perhaps have been expected of so unconventional a design, and Gresley reluctantly rebuilt it to a normal type 4-6-4, with conventional boiler in 1937; see Section 22, page 145.

2-6-2T (3-cyl) LNER Class V1/V3*, BR Power Class: 4MT (V3) 3MT (V1) Passenger Tank Engines

Introduced: 1930, 1939*

Total: 92†

For the intensive and heavily loaded suburban services in the Edinburgh area and between Glasgow and Helensburgh, a larger tank than the 'N2' 0-6-2Ts was needed by the late 1920s. Following his general big engine, three-cylinder policy, Gresley opted for a big 2-6-2T design. This wheel arrangement had shown itself to be an ideal one for such traffic, in particular on the GWR, and it was one which offered a significant increase in power and performance.

Prior to these engines being designed and built, a scheme had been drawn-up for a 2-6-2T design for use on the GN suburban traffic to Moorgate, but this was abandoned due to restrictions of track layout at Moorgate station (a similar scheme for a 2-6-4T also failed to materialise). The Scottish requirement was, however, filled by a 2-6-2T, the first of which appeared from Doncaster in October 1930, and which could be said to be a development of the design first outlined for the Moorgate services.

The three cylinders all drove on to the middle pair of coupled wheels, with the centre one steeply inclined at 1 in 8 to clear the leading coupled axle. A monobloc iron casting combined all three cylinders together. The general design features followed Gresley's standard practices at that time and included a side window cab similar to that produced for the 'K3' class; the design of the motion parts was also based upon the 'K3'.

†Original total: 82 Class V1 and 10 Class V3. Final total (after rebuilds): 19 Class V1 and 72 Class V3.

The engines were built as follows:

Nos 2900-2927	Doncaster	1930/31
Nos 2928-2933	Doncaster	1934/35
Nos 417/46/77/9/81/ 4/6/7/97/8, 402/ 14/5/6/8, 2897, 419/22/3/8/40, 2898 454/5/61/5/6, 2899	Doncaster	1935/36
Nos 404/7/20/4/5/47/8/ 51/67/9/72/8/80/3/5/ 8-91/6	Doncaster	1938/39
Nos 390-393/5-9, 401	Doncaster	1939/40

The final batch, delivered in 1939-40, had boilers with 200lb per sq in pressure, and were classified 'V3'. Subsequently 63 of the earlier engines received boilers of the higher pressure and these then also became Class V3. The haphazard numbering given to the class when new was replaced in 1946 by the numbers 7600-7691, in the order of building listed above. BR added 60000 to these numbers in 1948.

Below: The drawing depicts a later example of the 'V1' class, as built with a hopper coal bunker.

Top right: Class V1 2-6-2T No 2911, in black livery with red lining out, when new. Note the cut out in the cab roof over the entrance, and the open coal rails on the bunker. Photographed at Kings Cross in 1931 where it spent a month in the spring of that year on trials. The previous year No 2901 had been tried out on Marylebone suburban services. This broadside view gives an excellent impression of the handsome lines of these engines. *LPC*

Bottom right: Class V1 2-6-2T No 2930, photographed at Haymarket shed in 1938, showing the modified bunker without coal rails, and with a sheet steel top, with beading. Small destination board on smokebox door. Elbowed steam pipe covers. *Photomatic*

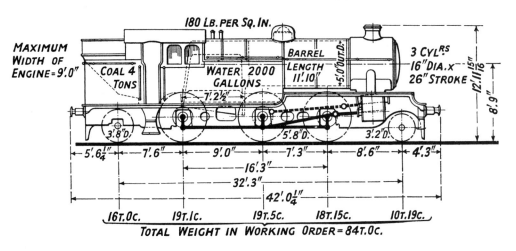

MAXIMUM WIDTH OF ENGINE = 9'.0"

180 LB. PER SQ. IN.

COAL 4 TONS

WATER 2000 GALLONS

BARREL LENGTH 11'.10"

5'.0" OUT.D.

3 CYL.RS 16" DIA. x 26" STROKE

12'.11 5/16"

8'.9"

7'.2 1/2"

3'.8"D.   5'.8"D.   3'.2"D.

5'.6 1/4"   7'.6"   9'.0"   7'.3"   8'.6"   4'.3"

16'.3"

32'.3"

42'.0 1/4"

16T.0c.   19T.1c.   19T.5c.   18T.15c.   10T.19c.

TOTAL WEIGHT IN WORKING ORDER = 84T.0c.

Top: No 2910 bustles along on semi-fast turn. *Ian Allan Library*

Above: Class V3 2-6-2T one of the 10 built new with 200lb per sq in boiler pressure and hopper type bunker, and no cutout in cab roof above entrance. Photographed in 1939, when new. Note the straight steam pipe covers. Subsequently 63 earlier locomotives were rebuilt to Class V3. *British Rail ER*

The bunker design was modified for the later engines, from 1936 onwards, to incorporate a coal hopper; previously the original coal rails had been changed to plain steel copings. Another feature of the later engines was the use of vacuum brakes for both engine and train, instead of steam for the engine and vacuum for the train. Twelve engines, sent to the GE Section, were given the Westinghouse air brake as well (see below).

These handsome engines proved to be excellent performers, and they were well liked by their Scottish drivers in particular, who kept their engines very well groomed. The Newcastle area received 25 of the class in 1935/36 and the 'V3's went to the NE area when new. Fifteen of the class were sent to the GE Section in 1938, (for some odd reason no Westinghouse brakes were fitted when delivered, and the first three never received them). In their final years they were often to be found on empty stock and parcels workings, as their passenger turns were replaced by diesel railcars.

Last of class withdrawn (V1): 67630/64/80 (1962)
(V3): 67620/8/36/8/40/3/6/78/84/90/1 (1964)
None preserved

Above: Class VI 2-6-2T No 481, at Newcastle Central in 1936. A curious feature of the front end of some of these locomotives was the provision of double guard irons; with two large ones bolted to the main frames and two small ones attached to the leading pony truck. *Photomatic*

Below: Also at Newcastle Central Class V1 2-6-2T No 497 is seen alongside ex NER Class A8 4-6-2T No 2154. The Gresley engine is in the plain wartime black livery, with the company initials abbreviated to NE. Sheet steel bunker top, with beading and two small brackets for headboard. *C. R. L. Coles*

The basic dimensions of the 'V1' class were as follows:

Heating surface, tubes
   Large and small: 1,198.0sq ft
   Firebox: 127.0sq ft
Total (evaporative): 1,325.0sq ft
Superheater: 284.0sq ft
   Combined heating surfaces: 1,609.0sq ft
   Superheater elements: 22
Grate area: 22.08sq ft
Tractive effort (at 85 per cent BP): 22,464.0lb
(The tractive effort of the Class V3 with 200lb per sq in boilers was 24,960lb)

Below: Postwar LNER apple green livery on Class V3 2-6-2T No 7684, with unshaded modified Gill Sans lettering and numerals; photographed at Gateshead shed in April 1947. This was the only engine of the class to carry green livery. *Photomatic*

Bottom: Twelve engines, sent to Stratford for work on the GE Section, were fitted with the Westinghouse air brake in addition to vacuum brakes. No 7669 is seen at Stratford in postwar plain black livery. One large guard iron missing from the front end. *E. R. Wethersett*

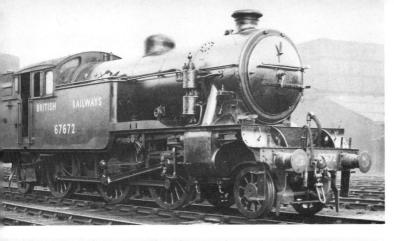

Top left: Westinghouse-fitted Class V3 No 67672, in early hybrid BR livery, at Stratford shed in July 1948. Number retained on tank sides in LNER fashion. *E. R. Wethersett*

Centre left: Also in the early BR livery of plain black with Gill Sans lettering and numerals, but No 67608 has the number relocated on the side of the bunker; a feature of the class in their final BR days. *J. Robertson*

Below: On shed at Haymarket, in March 1959, is Class V1 2-6-2T No 67610, still retaining the 180lb per sq in boiler, but with straight outside steam pipes and no cutout in cab roof. 63 engines of the 'V1' class were altered to 'V3s' between 1940 and 1961, making a total of 73 (the other 10 being built new as 'V3s'). This meant that 19 engines ran their entire lives as 'V1s'. *W. S. Sellar*

SECTION 19

2-8-2 (3-cyl) LNER Class P2
Heavy Passenger Engines
Introduced: 1934
Total: 6

For express passenger haulage on the Edinburgh-Aberdeen main line Gresley decided to exploit the high adhesion factor offered by the 2-8-2 wheel arrangement, rather than employ his Pacifics. The 2-8-2 still allowed a wide firebox to be used and he believed that the trailing wheels under the cab would assist in giving an acceptable riding quality on a route with heavy gradients and severe curvature. Gresley's interest in and admiration for his French contemporary, André Chapelon, did not extend to using the 4-8-0 layout that Chapelon had chosen for locomotives for similar duties, but it did show clearly in some of the design features of the new Class P2 2-8-2 locomotive No 2001 *Cock o' the North* as first introduced into service.

Cock o' the North was a remarkable engine in many ways, not least in appearance. Except for his own 'Hush-Hush' 4-6-4, no locomotive remotely resembling it had run on British rails before. Its outer form was the result of wind-tunnel experiments to ensure that exhaust smoke and steam would be thrown well clear of the cab. This requirement resulted in the cutaway top to the smokebox, enshrouded by two 'wings' extending forward each side from the boiler cladding; also the wedge-shaped front to the cab.

The French influence on No 2001 was readily apparent in the use of the ACFI feedwater heater, the Kylchap double blastpipe and chimney and (not visible to the naked eye) the enlarged, streamlined internal steam passages and ports. Gresley did not opt for the French preference for four-cylinder compounding however, choosing instead a three-cylinder simple layout operated by rotary cam poppet valves. The boiler was very similar to his

220lb per sq in Class A3 type, but had an increased grate area of 50sq ft.

A second engine, of basically similar outward appearance was delivered in October 1934; this was No 2002 *Earl Marischal*. This had some important design differences, in particular the use of piston valves and outside Walschaerts valve gear, with the Gresley derived motion for the middle cylinder. ACFI feedwater apparatus was not fitted. Experience in service soon showed that the softer exhaust of the piston valve engine required improved smoke deflection, and a second set of deflectors was fitted. This modification was never considered necessary for No 2001, whilst it ran with poppet valves.

The LNER sent No 2001 *Cock o' the North* to the Locomotive Testing Station at Vitry in France, for stationary trials on the rollers. At this time no equivalent testing plant was available to the LNER (although the GWR had one at Swindon), and Gresley was a fervent campaigner for the need for such facilities for his engine. No 2001 revealed certain weaknesses whilst on trial, but generally speaking it impressed the continental railwaymen, and the excellence of the workmanship and finish achieved by Doncaster was much admired.

By the time four more engines were ordered Gresley had settled for the piston valve layout, and had meanwhile produced his 'A4' Pacific design (see Section 20). For the four new Class P2 Mikados he applied the same pattern of streamlining that

Below: The drawing depicts the first of the class, No 2001 *Cock o' the North,* with rotary cam poppet valves; as first built. This was classified 'P2/1'.

Right: In this striking view of No 2001 *Cock o' the North,* taken when just completed, the cutaway and slope to the top of the smokebox is clearly seen, also the plain chimney for the Kylchap double blastpipe. The ACFI feedwater heater is visible on the running plate alongside the boiler. The class carried chime whistles. *British Rail ER*

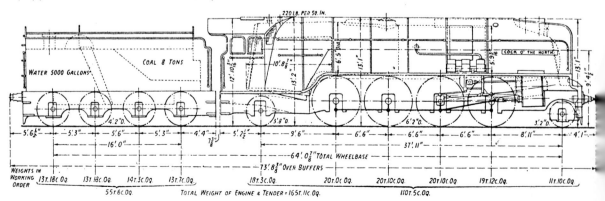

Above: Class P2 2-8-2 No 2002 *Cock o' the North,* in original condition, with rotary cam poppet valves and wing plates extending forward around the smokebox. The cab front was made wedge-shaped to give an improved lookout and aid the smoke deflection. *Photomatic*

Below: Fitted with an indicator shelter, during trial running, No 2001 *Cock o' the North* is seen here awaiting the road, at Kings Cross. The location of the whistle, in front of the chimney, was unusual in British practice. On one test from Kings Cross, before going into service, No 2001 worked a load of 19 vehicles of some 650 tons to Barkston and back, demonstrating a capacity for sustained hard work and free running when coasting. No 2001 went on exhibition at certain towns and cities on the LNER system, including Ilford and Aberdeen, before these trials from Kings Cross. *Ian Allan Library*

Top: In this rare photograph, taken by Bulleid, No 2001 stands in Amiens station, France. Note the large French style headlamps carried by the engine, which was en route to the locomotive testing station at Vitry-sur-Seine, having been shipped from Harwich on 4 December 1934. The engine was exhibited at the Gare du Nord, Paris alongside a Collin Super-Pacific. Tests at Vitry were not a great success, as the engine showed signs of overheating, and it was decided to continue the tests on the open road, using 'brake locomotives' behind the tender. The LNER wagons in the train contained a supply of British coal for the engine to use in France; to make test conditions as ideal as possible. *O. V. S. Bulleid*

Above: On shed during the controlled road tests, with locomotives attached behind the test carriage to act as 'brake locomotives'. These tests took place between Paris and St. Pierre-des-Corps on the Paris-Orleans line. Special brackets had to be added to the bufferbeam to carry the large headlights. *O. V. S. Bulleid*

Above: As described in the Introduction, on page 18, a second set of smoke deflectors was fitted to No 2002 *Earl Marischal,* to improve smoke lifting. These reduced the driver's forward vision quite considerably. The engine is seen here in this condition at Dundee shed. Note the speedometer drive from the rear coupled wheel. *Photomatic*

Right: The second Class P2 2-8-2, No 2002 *Earl Marischal,* with piston valves and Walschaerts valve gear; using Gresley's conjugated gear for the middle cylinder. The softer exhaust from this engine, compared with the poppet valve engine, led to complaints of inadequate smoke deflection. It was however, generally considered to be the better engine of the two so far as performance was concerned. This engine was classified 'P2/2'. *British Rail ER*

was carried by the 'A4's for the front end, although the boiler sides and layout of running plate behind the cylinders was more in keeping with the original 'P2' design, and not covered by a valance. This resulted in a singularly handsome looking design, combining graceful lines with a sense of power.

The 'A4'-type front end evidently proved more successful in exhaust clearance than the original design, and No 2002 was modified to receive the streamlined front in October 1936. More significantly, when No 2001 received this front end it also had the rotary cam poppet valves replaced by piston valves, and the ACFI apparatus was removed – thus becoming (in April 1938) a Class P2/2.

The engines were built as follows:

No 2001	Doncaster	1934
No 2002	Doncaster	1934
Nos 2003-2006	Doncaster	1936

In service, on the route for which they were specifically designed, the 'P2's gained something of a mixed reputation. The piston valve engines were definitely preferred to the poppet valve example (hence the conversion of No 2001), but the long coupled wheelbase on all the engines did not take kindly to the severe curvature of the route, and proved to be somewhat less flexible than was desirable. Breakages of steam pipes and heavy wear and overheating of motion parts and journals was a problem. They proved heavy on coal on the route, and the large grate was not popular with the firemen. On the credit side they were prodigiously powerful, and could seemingly haul any load required of them (without a significant increase in the already high coal consumption!). Some engineers openly expressed a preference for the Gresley Pacifics for the duties allocated to the Mikados, and the Class V2 2-6-2 also became popular.

When Edward Thompson succeeded Sir Nigel Gresley in 1941 he decided to rebuild the entire class as Pacifics; as described in Appendix 2.

Last of class rebuilt to Class A2/2 Pacific: No 2004 (1944)

The basic dimensions of the class were as follows:

Heating surface, tubes
  Large and small: 2,477.0sq ft
  Firebox: 237.0sq ft
Total (evaporative): 2,714.0sq ft
Superheater: 776.5sq ft
  Combined heating surfaces: 3,490.5sq ft
  Superheater elements: 43
Grate area: 50.0sq ft
Tractive effort (at 85 per cent BP): 43,462lb

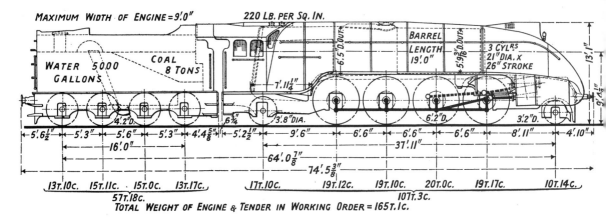

MAXIMUM WIDTH OF ENGINE = 9'.0" 220 LB. PER SQ. IN.

WATER 5000 GALLONS
COAL 8 TONS

BARREL LENGTH 19'.0"

3 CYLRS 21" DIA. X 26" STROKE

6'.5" D.OUT'R
5'.9 3/16" D.OUT'R

13'.1"
9'.4 1/4"

7'.11 1/4"
6 3/4"
3'.8" DIA.
4'.2"D.
6'.2"D.
3'.2"D.

5'.6 1/2" — 5'.3" — 5'.6" — 5'.3" — 4'.4 5/8" — 5'.2 1/2" — 9'.6" — 6'.6" — 6'.6" — 6'.6" — 8'.11" — 4'.10"

16'.0"
37'.11"
64'.0 7/8"
74'.5 3/8"

13T.10C. 15T.11C. 15T.0C. 13T.17C. 17T.10C. 19T.12C. 19T.10C. 20T.0C. 19T.17C. 10T.14C.
57T.18C.
107T.3C.

TOTAL WEIGHT OF ENGINE & TENDER IN WORKING ORDER = 165T.1C.

Above: The drawing depicts the later version of the Class P2 2-8-2s, with streamlined front end and piston valves.

Below: Application of the wedge-shaped streamlined front end to the 2-8-2s was most probably prompted by the problems experienced with smoke deflection on No

2002. The design was basically similar to what Gresley had introduced for his 'A4' Pacifics, except for a longer chimney casing to house the double Kylchap exhaust, except for No 2005 which had a smaller single blastpipe and chimney. No 2003 *Lord President* is seen, when new in June 1936, and on exhibition at Doncaster. Nos 2001/2 were rebuilt with streamlined noses in 1936/8 respectively, and the rest (Nos 2004-2006) were built new with them. *Ian Allan Library*

Top: The Aberdeen portion of the up 'Flying Scotsman' entering Edinburgh Waverley station on a very wet July day in 1938, headed by Class P2 2-8-2 No 2004 *Mons Meg.* *J. P. Wilson*

Above: The prototype engine as rebuilt with piston valves, Walschaerts valve gear and streamlined front end, in April 1938. The tender on No 2001 *Cock o' the North* was experimental, with all-welded construction for the body and spoked instead of disc wheels. The livery was the standard apple green, with black front end and cylinders. *NRM, Crown Copyright.*

Below: The final engine of the class, No 2006 *Wolf of Badenoch* had a modified boiler with the combustion chamber at the front of the firebox. No 2006 is seen here on shed at Haymarket. This engine was classified 'P2/3'. *T. G. Hepburn*

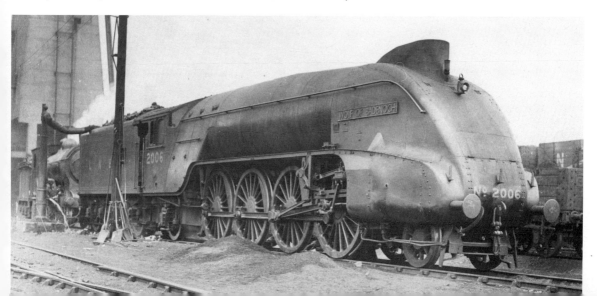

4-6-2 (3-cyl) LNER Class A4, BR Power Class 8P Express Passenger Engines
Introduced: 1935
Total: 34

The background story to the introduction of the outstandingly successful streamlined Class A4 Pacifics is given in the Introduction, and does not need to be repeated in detail here. It will suffice to add that an impressive effort was made by Doncaster works during the design and construction of the first engine. From receipt of the order and the start of the drawings on 28 March 1935, to completion and steaming of the engine was a period of only twenty-five weeks. (A similar effort was made for the new carriages for the 'Silver Jubilee' train, incidentally.)

No 2509 *Silver Link* made an immediate and lasting impression upon the public when it first appeared in September 1935. In appearance alone it departed radically from the accepted conventions of what a British express passenger steam locomotive should look like. This of course was because of the wedge-shaped front and the streamlined outer casing. O. S. Nock recounts that many connoisseurs of the graceful in locomotive lines were genuinely appalled by the new engine, although some later became reconciled to it.

Internally, the 'A4' had some significant new design features which were introduced specifically to suit the type of duty the engines would perform. The 'Silver Jubilee' train was to run to a schedule which involved fast timings on the level, with sustained speeds of 85-90mph and fast running uphill, with 70-75mph on gradients of 1 in 200. The load to be hauled, of only 235 tons gross, permitted these speeds in marked contrast to the heavier loads and correspondingly lower speeds of the Class A3 Pacifics over the same road. Therefore, compared to the 'A3's, the streamlined engines would be

working hardest at speeds of 75mph or more. The internal steam passages were streamlined, and the boiler pressure raised to 250lb per sq in. The piston valves were increased to 9in diameter and the cylinder bore was reduced from 19in to 18½in. There was a higher degree of superheat, and the boiler, which was a development of the 'A3' boiler, had the barrel shortened from 19ft to 18ft.

Silver Link quickly demonstrated its capabilities for high speed running, thrilling the public with news of a trial run on 27 September 1935 during which the engine twice reached 112½mph and ran no less than 43 miles at an average speed of 100mph – a feat accomplished when the engine was only three weeks old.

Four engines were built for the 'Silver Jubilee' train, with three allocated to Kings Cross and one to Gateshead, as a spare engine. As first built these four, Nos 2509-2512 had a bulbous streamlined nose with short buffer stocks and a recessed housing for the front coupling; Doncaster later made the streamlined nose more pointed, and fitted longer buffers and an exposed coupling hook. Livery for the four engines was silver-grey, with the smokebox, front, valances and frames in a darker grey. Wheels were silver-grey, and the lettering was silver with a blue background.

So successful were the four engines in everyday service that the LNER Board's Joint Locomotive & Traffic Committee authorised construction of a further 17 as part of a locomotive renewal programme for 1936 onwards. Significantly hardly any change had to be made to their design except some small details and a change of livery. At first standard apple green replaced the silver grey, but when it was decided to introduce further stream-

Below: Class A4 Pacific, with single blastpipe and chimney, and corridor tender, in original prewar condtion with valances over coupled wheels.

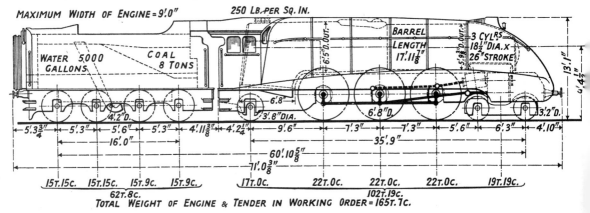

Above: Class A4 4-6-2 No 2511 *Silver King* in original condition in silver grey and dark grey livery, with painted name on the centre of the boiler casing. Original front end, with short buffers, and coupling housed in a recess in the casing. This front end layout was modified following an accident at Kings Cross when a man was trapped and hurt, due to insufficient clearance between the buffers when compressed. *W. J. Reynolds*

Centre left: Also showing how the front coupling was originally recessed in a housing (and with the short buffers fitted) No 2512 *Silver Fox* makes a striking picture speeding at 80mph at the head of the up 'Silver Jubilee', past Oakleigh Park. This particular engine had a stainless steel replica of a fox beneath the name, and had polished steel boiler bands and handrails. The locomotive and train were both finished in the silver (or more correctly – aluminium grey) livery and the front end and valance of the locomotive, also the engine and tender frames, were in a darker grey. The wheels were also silver, with grey tyres, and the lettering and numerals were in a lighter silver, with blue shading. The front of the locomotive carried no number, to begin with. *F. R. Hebron*

Bottom left: No 2509 *Silver Link,* first of the class to be delivered, but seen here after the front end had been modified, with the streamline casing taken back to a less pointed profile, with new extended buffers and without a recess for the front coupling. Note the horizontal handrail on the boiler side; all others had a curved handrail, (No 2509 was later modified to match). *Silver Link* was photographed under the coaling plant at York, in July 1936. Small shaded numerals for number added to the front end of the locomotive. *Photomatic*

lined high speed services for 1937, which was to be Coronation year, a new livery of garter blue was applied to seven engines required to operate the 'Coronation' and the 'West Riding Limited'. Eventually, the existing silver grey and green engines were also repainted blue, with dark indian red wheels. The final locomotive of this batch of 17 was the 100th Gresley Pacific completed by Doncaster, and it was ceremonially named *Sir Nigel Gresley* at Marylebone station on 26 November 1937. (Gresley had been knighted in recognition of his services the previous year.)

A further 14 engines were authorised and followed on in construction; of these, four differed in having Kylchap double exhausts with large double chimney. These were Nos 4468, 4901-4903, introduced in 1938, and it was soon evident to Gresley that these were particularly fine steamers. Nevertheless because of the outbreak of war and

Gresley's death, it was not until BR days that the rest of the class were similarly treated, from May 1957 onwards, thereby boosting their performance.

It was one of the freer-running Kylchap engines, No 4468 *Mallard*, that established the steam locomotive speed record of 126mph whilst engaged

Below: The four 'Silver' engines were followed by an order for 17 more 'A4s'. The first of these, No 4482 *Golden Eagle,* was completed at the end of 1936, and emerged in LNER apple green livery with black front end, valances and frames lined out in red. The name was moved forward to the smokebox side and carried on a cast brass plate. The corridor tender fitted was originally built in 1928 for the Class A1/A3 Pacifics and was modified with streamline fairings on the top, for use with the 'A4'. Note the rubber sheeting between cab roof and tender top. *British Rail ER*

Right: For Class A4 Pacifics Nos 4483-4487 a variation of the apple green livery was applied, with the whole front casing painted black as far back as the rear of the smokebox. No 4487 *Sea Eagle* is seen here in the paint shop at Doncaster in April 1937. The colour scheme in this form did not enhance the graceful lines of the engine. *Photomatic*

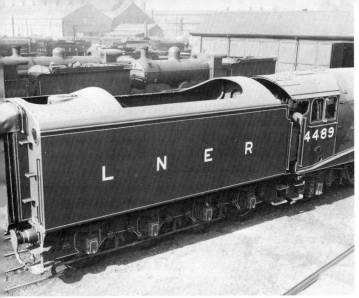

Top left: No 4489 *Woodcock* was finished in shop-grey paint, with white lining and lettering; and ran in traffic for some two weeks in this state, in May 1937. The tender attached (seen in the short-lived shop-grey livery) was a 1928 corridor tender, originally produced for the Class A1/A3 Pacifics, which was modified with streamlined sides and fairings around the coal space and tank filler. The rubber sheeting between cab roof and tender top was not yet fitted when this picture was taken in Doncaster works yard. *British Rail ER*

Centre left: The down 'Coronation' passing Ganwick, headed by No 4489 *Dominion of Canada* (originally named *Woodcock*). The 'Coronation' train had new carriages finished in garter blue below the waist and Marlborough blue above, and to match this scheme seven of the new Class A4 Pacifics were painted in garter blue, with black front and frames (lining between the blue and black was vermilion and straw), and dark Indian red wheels. Lettering and numerals were in polished steel Gill Sans (except the front number which was painted on) and many fittings, such as the cab window frames, were chromium plated. *F. R. Hebron*

Below: The five Class A4 Pacifics normally allocated to the 'Coronation' service were given the names of constituents of the British Empire, and following official ceremonies, they carried the armorial bearings of the countries concerned beneath the number on the cabside. In addition three of them had special whistles, as follows: No 4488, a South African Railways chime whistle; No 4489, a Canadian Pacific Railroad five-chime whistle, and No 4492 a deep-toned New Zealand Government Railways whistle. In 1938 No 4489 *Dominion of Canada* was presented with a standard CPR locomotive bell, which was mounted on a special bracket forward of the chimney. *British Rail ER*

Right: Class A4 Pacific No 4491 *Commonwealth of Australia* at speed with the 'Coronation' express. The articulated carriages produced by Gresley for this train had rubber fairings between carriage ends and valances between the wheels, to assist in giving an aerodynamic form to the whole ensemble. *E. R. Wethersett*

Below: Although Nos 4488-4492 were delivered in garter blue for the 'Coronation' service, Nos 4493-94 were painted green when new. By the time the next batch of Class A4s were ready, the decision had been taken to paint the whole class garter blue, including the original silver engines. Some of the garter blue engines carried polished steel lettering and numerals but others, such as No 4467 *Wild Swan,* seen here leaving Kings Cross at the head of the 'Northern Belle' cruising train, had the standard gold shaded red and black transfers, as carried by the apple green engines. *LPC*

Above: Surprisingly little modification was made to the Class A4 Pacific design, as new construction proceeded, until 1938 when Gresley fitted Kylchap double blast pipes and double chimneys to four locomotives, Nos 4468, 4901-4903. This necessitated a considerably larger streamlined outer casing to the chimney, as can be seen here on No 4468 *Mallard,* seen when new at the head of the up 'Yorkshire Pullman' near Brookmans Park. This picture was taken prior to *Mallard's* epic record-breaking run of 3 July 1938, when it attained a world speed record for steam traction of 126mph. *Ian Allan Library*

Centre right: Two Class A4s named for the 'West Riding' service, No 4495 *Golden Fleece* in the background, with the front end of No 4496 *Golden Shuttle* in the foreground at Kings Cross locomotive yard. *Golden Fleece* carried the name *Great Snipe* for about a month when new, in August 1937, and *Golden Shuttle* was renamed *Dwight D. Eisenhower* in September 1945. *Photomatic*

Bottom right: Another of the Kylchap-fitted Class A4s, No 4901 *Capercaillie* (later renamed *Charles H. Newton* and finally *Sir Charles Newton*) seen here at the head of a down express at York in August 1939. Garter blue livery, with standard shaded lettering and numerals. *Photomatic*

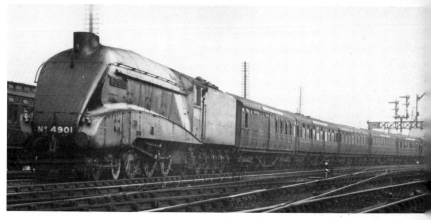

in special high speed train braking trials on 3 July 1938.

The engines were built as follows:

Nos 2509-2512	Doncaster	1935
Nos 4482-4498	Doncaster	1936/37
Nos 4462-4469	Doncaster	1937/38
4499-4500		
4900-4903		

Under the first 1946 renumbering scheme, the engines of the class were to become Nos 580-613 (in order of building) but only Nos 4483/5/6, 4466 actually carried the numbers 585/7/8, 605 respectively, before the introduction of the second 1946 renumbering scheme, when the class became Nos 1-34. This renumbering was not in building sequence and is shown below for convenience of reference.

Below: The outbreak of World War 2 brought an abrupt charge to the careers of the Class A4 Pacifics. The colourful and glamorous streamlined trains were put into store, and the locomotives themselves put to work on heavily laden passenger trains, where sheer haulage power took precedence over speed capabilities. The need for ease of maintenance and repair led to the removal of the streamlined valances ahead of the cylinders and over the coupled wheels, to expose the motion. (One engine,

No 4462, retained the front end valance only, for a while). The livery became plain black overall, and the company initials were abbreviated to NE, using the shaded transfers. No 4901 is seen after renaming to *Charles H. Newton,* and it makes an interesting comparison with the preceding picture of the same locomotive in prewar days. Chime whistle replaced by standard LNER loco whistle. *British Rail ER*

Right: The German air raid on the City of York on 29 April 1942 resulted in a direct hit on the locomotive sheds, where Class A4 Pacific No 4469 *Sir Ralph Wedgwood* (formerly *Gadwall*) received the full blast of a bomb. The engine was wrecked beyond economic repair, and withdrawn in June of that year, but the tender was salvaged and in postwar years it ran attached to Class A2/1 Pacific No 3696. *British Rail ER*

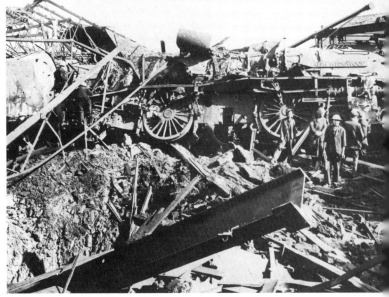

Original Number:	LNER 1946 Number:	Original Number:	LNER 1946 Number:
2509	14	4496	8
2510	15	4497	31
2511	16	4498	7
2512	17	4462	4
4482	23	4463	18
4483	24	4464	19
4484	25	4465	20
4485	26	4466	6
4486	27	4467	21
4487	28	4468	22
4488	9	4469	*
4489	10	4499	2
4490	11	4500	1
4491	12	4900	32
4492	13	4901	5
4493	29	4902	33
4494	3	4903	34
4495	30		

*No 4469 was destroyed during an air raid at York in 1942 and not replaced.

Above left: Still in wartime black livery, but with full initials restored to the tender side, and commendably clean, No 2511 *Silver King* is seen here in early postwar days, with chime whistle restored. *E. R. Wethersett*

Left: As early as September 1945 one Class A4 Pacific was restored to garter blue livery. This was undertaken specially for the renaming of No 4496 as *Dwight D. Eisenhower,* and no further engines were painted blue for a further nine months or more. From mid-August 1946 onwards the class received garter blue as they passed through the works for repair, and (because of the 1946 renumbering scheme, in which they became Nos 1-34) they were given new cut-out metal Gill Sans numerals and lettering. No 1 *Sir Ronald Mathews* is seen on the turntable at Grantham, carrying the 'Flying Scotsman' headboard. *T. G. Hepburn*

Right: Like the majority of locomotives, the Class A4 Pacifics were in a pretty poor shape by the end of the war, and the early postwar phase did not see much of a general improvement. Lack of engine cleaners is all too evident in the sad appearance of No 10 *Dominion of Canada,* heading a vans train near Bradman's Box. Comparison with the picture of the same locomotive on page 125 is too odious for words! *M. W. Earley*

Top right: At Reading shed on 28 April 1948, No E22 *Mallard* prepares to return to the Eastern Region, after running trials on the Western Region that month. The prefix E to the number and the new title 'British Railways' carried in painted Gill Sans lettering were temporary expedients pending the new Regional number schemes for the nationalised system. The trial runs were part of the famous 1948 locomotive interchange trials organised as a prelude to the design of new standard locomotive designs for all the BR system. World speed record commemorative plaque on boiler side. *M. W. Earley*

Centre right: Topping Camden bank on the climb out of Euston is Class A4 Pacific No 60034 *Lord Farringdon* at the head of the 10am down 'Royal Scot' express, complete with the LMSR dynamometer car (leading vehicle), on 25 May 1948, during the locomotive interchange trials organised by British Railways. *F. R. Hebron*

Right: Another view of No 60034 *Lord Farringdon* at the head of the down 'Royal Scot' on 25 May 1948, passing over Dillicar troughs at speed. *Overend Press*

Below: For the 1948 locomotive interchange trials the three Class A4 Pacifics selected to take part received 1928-style corridor tenders in place of the non-corridor type with which they were originally fitted. Because the water columns at Euston station had low slung arms, the backs of the corridor tenders had to be cut down, as seen here on the tender of No E22 *Mallard* photographed during coaling-up at Nine Elms shed, whilst running on the Southern. *Eric Treacy*

The tenders attached to the 'A4's were a mixed selection, and included the original 1928 corridor tenders built for the 'A3's, suitably streamlined in 1937 for their new role. In addition new corridor and non-corridor tenders were built. Roller bearing axleboxes were fitted to three tenders in 1938/9, with Hoffman, Skefko and Timken types used for comparison.

Wartime provided the complete antithesis to the ideal operating conditions for the high speed 'A4' Pacifics, and it soon became apparent that these sophisticated machines then demanded more than their fair quota of time for maintenance and repair. Before his untimely death in 1941, Gresley had already started to consider ways of improving their availability, in particular by eliminating the troubles which in these conditions, revealed themselves in the design of the big end, and in the wear on the conjugated three-cylinder gear. Gresley's successor Edward Thompson wanted to replace the conjugated gear completely with three separate sets of Walschaerts valve gear, but this scheme never came to fruition. He did, however remove the streamlined side valances over the coupled wheels, in order to make the existing motion more accessible for maintenance, and he made a number of other detail changes, with the same aim in mind.

Faced with loads far above those they had been designed to haul, the 'A4's now revealed both their true strength and their true weaknesses. Wartime passenger trains of from 600 to 750 tons were a regular feature of the Kings Cross departure platforms. These had to be taken from a dead stand, through the tunnels and up the initial grades of 1 in 105-110, without assistance, so Thompson decided to alter the valve motion to increase the maximum

cut-off of 75 per cent instead of 65 per cent; commencing with No 4499 in March 1943. This proved successful, but the prevailing day-to-day conditions did not allow for a speedy conversion programme, and only 12 locomotives were altered by 1948. However, BR continued the policy and all 34 were converted by May 1957.

As we have already seen, Gresley wanted to convert the entire class to the Kylchap double blastpipe arrangement. Certainly this conversion would have assisted the general performance of the engines in early postwar days, when the poor coal available (even to top-link engines) led to many minor ailments, and to poor running and poor steaming, but this conversion was not to take place before 1957/58, by which time improved attention to the valve gear was another feature of Doncaster practice. In their final years the 'A4's were in fine fettle, with a marked increase in mileage between heavy repairs, and with remarkably few failures in day-to-day service. In the first phase of the BR Modernisation Plan they were able to deputise for

Below: In the first year of nationalisation a number of experimental liveries were tried out on selected engines and trains, to test public opinion. In June/July 1948, four Class A4 Pacifics had their garter blue livery replaced by a deep ultramarine (almost purple in shade) with red, cream and grey LNWR-style lining. These four were Nos 60024/7/8/9. Note that the lining followed the form of the valance ahead of the cylinders. No 60029 *Woodcock* is seen passing the site of the old Holloway station, climbing the bank with the down 'Flying Scotsman' on 27 August 1948. *British Rail ER*

Top: In the standard BR light blue livery finally selected, with black and white lining, but in this instance without lettering or crest on the tender, Class A4 Pacific No 60009 *Union of South Africa* is just about to depart from Kings Cross at the head of the 'Capitals Limited'. This blue livery was abandoned in August 1951, on the grounds that it did not wear well in service, and was replaced by the dark Brunswick green. *Eric Treacy*

Above: Class A4 Pacific No 60028 *Walter K. Whigham* is seen returning tender-first from Hitchin to Finsbury Park with the Pullman cars of the 'Queen of Scots' on 23

February 1957 after trials with BR aws equipment. It was rare indeed to see an 'A4' working tender-first, other than as a light engine. Note the express train headcode carried. *M. Thompson*

Below: Going in fine style at the head of the up 'Norseman' is Class A4 No 60017 *Silver Fox,* seen passing Retford goods yard on 23 August 1952. The engine is in the final livery of dark Brunswick green, and the train is painted in the standard carmine red and cream livery; not a very pleasing combination. *T. Lewis*

Above: By the mid 1950s the Class A4s had been restored to fine fettle, with a number of detail modifications, and with greatly improved routine maintenance schedules. Perhaps the greatest single improvement was the fitting, at low cost, of Kylchap double exhausts to the entire class (except of course the four that were built new with them, see p127). This took place between May 1957 and the end of 1958. Seen in immaculate condition, at Hornsey on 23 October 1964 is No 60009 *Union of South Africa,* with BR aws equipment below bufferbeam area, with shield to protect it from the coupling. Note the plate on boiler side (left hand side only) depicting a Springbok; presented to the engine by a Bloemfontein newspaper proprietor in 1953. *G. Wheeler*

Below: General overhauls for two Class A4 Pacifics in Doncaster works in June 1960. On the left is No 60012 *Commonwealth of Australia* and on the right No 60008 *Dwight D. Eisenhower.* The smokebox door proper is visible on No 60012, inside the casing. *Colin P. Walker*

Above: To gain access to the smokebox door, hidden within the casing, two opening doors in the casing were provided; these opened upwards and downwards as is seen here on No 60034 *Lord Farringdon* photographed at Aberdeen Ferryhill shed, being prepared to work a Glasgow express in July 1966. *B. Lister*

Centre right: Several variations in tender design were employed with the 'A4s', and these of course became interchanged with the passage of time. For the initial four 'Silver' engines, new corridor tenders with streamlined finish were built, which has curved rear ends to match the standard LNER carriage end. One of these, minus the streamlined fairings which were originally a feature of the top of the tender, is seen attached to No 60017 *Silver Fox* in BR days. Further details of the tender design variations can be found on page 131. Photographed at York. *Eric Treacy*

Bottom right: Class A4 Pacific No 60027 *Merlin* caught by the camera leaving Perth on the 10am Dundee-Glasgow train on 23 July 1964. The plaque carried on the boiler side was presented by *HMS Merlin* (an Admiralty shore establishment) in May 1946. Originally the plaques were carried on the cab sides, but were moved to the boiler in 1948 during a routine works overhaul. Note BR speedometer drive from rear coupled wheel, and final style of BR Lion and wheel emblem transfer on tender side. *Paul Riley*

many a failed main line diesel, and to cope with the new loads and schedules demanded of them. Speeds of 100mph were by no means the exception, despite their age.

A final fling enjoyed by the 'A4's was the transfer of some of the class to the Scottish Region (once the 'Deltics' had finally displaced them from the Eastern Region) where they were well employed, and enthusiastically worked by their crews, on the Glasgow-Aberdeen services.

Below: Time inevitably took its toll of the streamlined casings on the 'A4' Pacifics, and No 60019 *Bittern* was beginning to show its true age by the time this picture was taken in September 1966 at St Rollox shed, Glasgow, in the early hours of the morning. Nevertheless, although some of the paintwork has been burned-off the casing, the engine was well polished and evidently well cared for. By this time diesels were the usual shed neighbours, and the days of the fabulous 'A4s' were strictly numbered. Note the drive to the mechanical lubricators, taken off the rear coupled wheels. BR overhead 25kV catenary warning notices attached to the boiler casing. *J. R. Carter*

Understandably, the Gresley 'A4's have been popular candidates for preservation, with no less than six engines retained for posterity. Two of these have gone overseas, to Canada: (No 60010 *Dominion of Canada,* Montreal Railway Historical Museum) and to the United States: (No 60008 *Dwight D. Eisenhower,* at Green Bay, Wisconsin, National Railroad Musuem).

Last of class withdrawn: 60019/24 (1966)
Examples preserved: 60007/8/9/10/9/22

Typical dimensions of the 'A4' class in LNER days were as follows:

Heating surface, tubes
 Large and small: 2,345.1sq ft
 Firebox: 231.2sq ft
Total (evaporative): 2,576.3sq ft
Superheater: 748.9sq ft
 Combined heating surfaces: 3,325.2sq ft
 Superheater elements: 43
Grate area: 41.25sq ft
Tractive effort (at 85 per cent BP): 35,455lb

Above: The down 3.0pm 'Scots Goods' with Class A4 Pacific No 60028 *Walter K. Whigham* in charge, seen passing Hadley Wood in September 1960. Locomotive in final form, with Kylchap double blastpipe and chimney and BR aws fitted. *Derek Cross*

Below: The final days of the magnificent 'A4' Pacifics found them working on the Glasgow-Aberdeen road, where they were much appreciated by the enginemen. No 60034 *Lord Farringdon* makes a splendid picture as it leaves Aberdeen on the 1.30pm to Glasgow on 28 January 1966, with chime whistle in full cry. *Paul Riley*

SECTION 21

2-6-2 (3-cyl) LNER Class V2, BR Power Class 6MT
Heavy Mixed-Traffic Engines
Introduced: 1936
Total: 184

By the mid-1930s the express passenger engines of the LNER were sufficiently numerous and successful to place that aspect of the company's services well to the fore, in their everyday railway operations. The steady growth of road transport competition for goods traffic, however, still required a determined effort on the part of the management and a new scheme for express parcels traffic was introduced, called the 'Green Arrow'. Suitable locomotives to run these fast goods services were either the Pacifics (needed for other work) or the 'K3' 2-6-0s. The 'K3s' were however rough riders at the relatively high speeds envisaged, and by 1935 the LNER had announced its intention to build a new type of locomotive for 'heavy long-distance work'.

One idea was for an articulated 2-6-4-4 version of the 'K3', and after this was rejected schemes for a 4-6-0 and a 2-6-2 were examined. The latter wheel arrangement was selected, and the 'V2' class was created on the Doncaster drawing boards. The first of the class to emerge, in June 1936, was appropriately named *Green Arrow*. Only five engines were built to begin with, and these were allocated to widely different areas of the LNER system, in order to gain operating experience with them. Although of heavy mixed-traffic concept, the 'V2' was also suitable for express passenger duties on account of the relatively large coupled wheel diameter of 6ft 2in. An interesting feature of the design was the wide spacing of the coupled wheels, compared to the Pacifics, and the overall coupled wheelbase was slightly longer. The weight of the Class V2 was such that they were restricted to main line duties for the most part, so therefore cannot be regarded as a true versatile mixed-traffic design of the type epitomised by the Stanier 'Black Five' or the WR 'Hall'. It was left to Gresley's successor, Thompson, to fill this need with the 'B1' class two-cylinder 4-6-0.

Most features of the Class V2 were well-proven on previous Gresley types, and the 2-to-1 conjugated gear was used, placed ahead of the cylinders. The cylinders themselves were a monobloc casting which also incorporated the steamchests, smokebox saddle and outside steampipes. A shortened version of the 'A3' boiler was designed, and the 'banjo' steam collector replaced the conventional dome. The large cab had the wedge shaped front which was proven to be effective in deflecting exhaust away from the driver's vision. The running plate was raised sufficiently high to clear the coupled wheels and eliminate the need for splashers. A standard six-wheeled 4,200 gallon tender was fitted.

In effect the Class V2 was like a shortened Pacific, with a pony truck replacing the leading bogie, and in service they quickly demonstrated an ability to run fast with heavy loads, on passenger trains as well as the express goods. With their conjugated three-cylinder motion in good fettle they were virtually the equal of the 'A3' Pacifics, but once wear set in, or the setting of the valves was astray, they had to be flogged to keep to Pacific schedules. The sounds they produced in worn condition echoed for many a mile around the lineside, as the author can vividly recall to this day!

Below: Class V2 2-6-2 heavy mixed-traffic design, as first constructed.

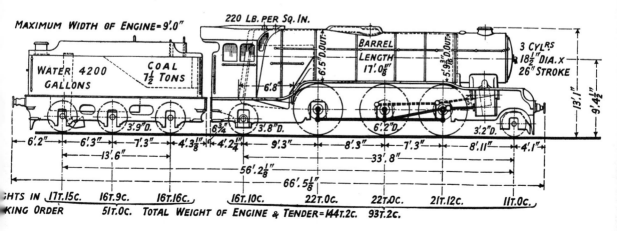

MAXIMUM WIDTH OF ENGINE = 9'.0"

220 LB. PER SQ. IN.

WATER 4200 GALLONS

COAL 7½ TONS

BARREL LENGTH 17'.0⅛"

3 CYLRS 18½" DIA. x 26" STROKE

GHTS IN 17T.15C.   16T.9C.   16T.16C.   16T.10C.   22T.0C.   22T.0C.   21T.12C.   11T.0C.

KING ORDER   51T.0C.   TOTAL WEIGHT OF ENGINE & TENDER = 144T.2C.   93T.2C.

Above: Class V2 2-6-2 No 4771 *Green Arrow* in full apple green livery, makes a beautiful picture when new, at the head of a fast fitted goods of the type the engine was specifically named after. Note the container wagons at the head of the train. The nameplate on this engine (which was to have been numbered 637) was originally to have been curved and placed above the coupled wheels, but Gresley changed it to a straight one and to the smokebox location before it went into traffic with the number 4771.
P. Ransome-Wallis

Centre right: One of the named examples, No 4780 *The Snapper,* photographed at York in July 1938. The nameplate carried the inscription 'The East Yorkshire Regiment – The Duke of York's Own' and had the regimental colours and badge on the backing plate. Only 8 Class V2s were named out of the class total of 184.
Photomatic

Bottom right: The rakish good looks of the Class V2 design remained evident from almost every angle, not least this one, where the wedge-shaped cab front effectively blends with the rake-back of the firebox from the boiler. The banjo dome and elegant curved running plate gave added emphasis to the overall impression of power and grace. No 4794 is seen at Grantham in 1939. *Photomatic*

Above: Another of the named engines, No 4806 *The Green Howard,* with regimental colours and badge and with the inscription *'Alexandra, Princess of Wales's Own Yorkshire Regiment'.* Old pattern 'Group Standard' tender with stepped-out copings, and MLS multiple-valve regulator fitted, with external rods along the boiler side to the smokebox; a feature of Nos 4804/6. *LPC*

Below: On a hot June day in 1939, Class V2 2-6-2 No 4830 is seen heading a Nottingham-Marylebone excursion train near Princes Risborough. This was a Leicester-based engine which was mainly intended for use on the overnight Marylebone-Newcastle trains. *H. K. Harman*

The engines were built as follows:

Nos 4771-4775	Doncaster	1936
Nos 4776-4803	Darlington	1937/38
Nos 4804-4814	Darlington	1938
Nos 4815-4842	Darlington	1939
Nos 4843-4852	Doncaster	1939/40
Nos 4853-4888	Darlington	1939/40
Nos 4889-4898	Darlington	1941
Nos 3655-3664	Doncaster	1941/42
No 4899	Darlington	1941
Nos 3641-3695	Darlington	1942-1944

In the first 1946 renumbering scheme, the following engines carried their new numbers for a while:

Nos 4780/1/2/5/9/90/1/2/3, 4800/21/33/42/66/70/76/80, 3683 which became Nos 709/10/1/4/18/9/20/1/2/9/50/62/71/95/9, 805/9/71 in the same order.

The second 1946 renumbering scheme placed the class as Nos 800-893 in the order of building listed above. BR added 60000 to these numbers in 1948.

As can be seen from the building dates shown above, construction of the Class V2s was carried on through the war years, with the final one, No 3695,

Top right: On a down express near Bell Bar in 1945, No 4896 is seen in wartime plain black livery, with the abbreviated initials NE on the tender. The engines were called upon to perform some remarkable feats of haulage during World War 2, including one of the heaviest locomotive-hauled passenger trains ever to run in Britain, a load of 26 coaches, weighing 860 tons gross, which No 4800 hauled from Peterborough to London (76.4 miles) in 102 minutes. *Photomatic*

Centre right: Photographed at Peterborough in April 1946, Class V2 2-6-2 No 729, in plain black livery, demonstrates the shortlived renumbering scheme applied to some of the class. Later in 1946 this engine became No 829, having started life as No 4800. *H. C. Casserley*

Below: Class V2 2-6-2 No 853 makes a fine study at the head of a vintage GNR quintuple articulated suburban set, seen passing Beeston Junction on a Leeds-Doncaster working, shortly before nationalisation. In postwar LNER days the class remained in black livery except for one example, No 4854, which was painted apple green. *Eric Treacy*

being completed at Darlington in June 1944. This was a tribute to their general usefulness at a time when most locomotive construction was restricted to heavy goods engines of the 2-8-0 type. Indeed, it was in the grim war years that the 'V2s' really showed their immense strength. On one occasion a load of 26 coaches was hauled by No 4800, from Peterborough to London.

The early postwar years understandably found the class in a somewhat less than ex-works condition, but a gradual improvement in maintenance was effected and generally speaking, by the mid-1950s the 'V2s' were once again showing their fine capabilities in everyday use. A development which came too late to be widely applied was the fitting of a Kylchap double blastpipe and chimney, in place of the original single chimney; only five engines were fitted before the new diesels came to the fore in BR affairs, and development work on steam was officially halted.

Last of class withdrawn: 60836 (1965)
Example preserved: LNER No 4771 *Green Arrow*

The basic dimensions of the class were as follows:

Heating surface, tubes
    Large and small: 2,216.07sq ft
    Firebox: 215.0sq ft
Total (evaporative): 2,431.07sq ft
Superheater: 679.67sq ft
    Combined heating surfaces: 3,110.74sq ft
    Superheater elements: 43
Grate area: 41.25sq ft
Tractive effort (at 85 per cent BP): 33,730lb

Above: Before the BR numbering scheme was finalised (under which all ex LNER engines had 60000 added to their existing running numbers), a few engines were given the prefix E to their number, to denote Eastern Region. No E851, with tender lettered 'British Railways' and in plain black livery, was photographed at Aberdeen in June 1949. *H. C. Casserley*

Left: In 1947 No 813 was fitted with a small stovepipe chimney and a curious trough-type smoke deflector – giving the front end a distinctly odd appearance. In very grubby condition the engine is seen here at the bufferstops at Kings Cross, shortly after receiving the modification. *C. C. B. Herbert*

Below: British Railways decided to paint the class in the standard BR mixed-traffic livery of black lined-out in LNWR-style with red, cream and grey. An early recipient, seen here, was No 60969, which was painted before the lion and wheel totem had been chosen for the tender sides. The engine is seen arriving at Tay Bridge station, Dundee, at the head of a goods train in February 1950. In their final years on BR the class were all given Brunswick green livery with orange and black livery. *E. M. Patterson*

Bottom: A remarkable event took place in the summer of 1953, when as a result of the discovery of a serious defect, the Southern Region had temporarily to withdraw from service its Bulleid 'Merchant Navy' Pacifics. To cover the locomotive shortage other Regions loaned engines to the SR, and amongst these were some ER Class V2 2-6-2s. Looking very presentable, No 60893 is seen at the head of the 'Bournemouth Belle' Pullman Car train, at Southampton Central. *E. Elsey*

Above: A Gresley Class V2 2-6-2 was selected by BR for testing at the Swindon Plant and on the road. Here the engine is seen during the road trials with the WR dynamometer car and front end indicator shelter, and with a coal cage on the tender. A 20-coach load was being pulled with the speed deliberately reduced by braking to 15-20mph for test purposes, on a 1 in 300 gradient at Badminton, during a run from Stoke Gifford to Reading. *P. M. Alexander*

Below: No 60813 retained its odd stovepipe chimney and smoke deflector device until its withdrawal. Here the engine is seen in BR green livery, beautifully groomed and with silver painted buffers and smokebox details, photographed leaving Dundee with an afternoon freight to Perth in August 1966. BR aws gear fitted below bufferbeam, with shield for the coupling. *S. C. Crook*

Above: Towards the end of their days, if a Class V2 required cylinder replacement, the original monobloc casting was replaced by three separate cast cylinders, and outside steampipes were fitted. Also five engines were given Kylchap double blastpipes and chimneys. These were Nos 60858/902/3 (with original cylinders) and Nos 60862/81 (with new cylinders); No 60862 is seen here at Grantham shed in August 1962. *K. R. Pirt*

Below: Class V2 2-6-2 No 60847 picks up speed on its way out of York at the head of the 11.30am train to Newcastle, in August 1964. Speedometer fitted, with drive from rear coupled axle; new outside steampipes with separate cast cylinders, and BR aws gear fitted. *Colin P. Walker*

SECTION 22

4-6-4 (3-cyl) LNER Class W1 (Rebuilt*), BR Power Class 8P
Express Passenger Engine
Introduced: 1937
Total: 1

After a prolonged spell of storage in a siding at Darlington, the high-pressure Class W1 4-6-4 (see Section 17, page 104) was removed to Doncaster in 1937. There it was reconstructed and reboilered, and given the standard Gresley conjugated three-cylinder layout, a Kylchap double blastpipe and chimney, an 'A4'-type streamlined nose and casing and a wedge-shaped cab. New cylinders were fitted, and the new boiler was of similar dimensions to that provided for the Class P2 2-8-2s, with a similar large grate area of 50sq ft. The original 4-6-4 wheel arrangement was retained, allowing for a particularly spacious cab. The original numbering of 10000 was also retained, and the engine was finished in

*Rebuilt from Gresley/Yarrow high pressure engine.

the garter blue livery then standard for the Class A4 Pacifics, but alone of all the steamliners, it never carried a name.

With a tractive effort of 41,435lb, the 4-6-4 was a remarkably powerful engine, but for some reason (probably due to the restricted size of the piston valves used) it did not demonstrate the very high speed propensities of the 'A4' Pacifics. In sheer haulage ability it was, however, superb, and was

Below: The drawing depicts the Class W1 4-6-4 as rebuilt with a conventional boiler, streamlined casing and Kylchap double blastpipe and chimney.

Bottom: The long and elegant lines of No 10000 as rebuilt with a streamlined casing and conventional boiler are readily apparent in this broadside study of the engine which was taken just after rebuilding in 1937. The cab was particularly large and spacious, due to the length of the frames at the rear of the firebox. Because of the somewhat unusual layout of the two trailing wheels, (one with outside and one with inside, journals) the technical press of the day sometimes referred to No 10000 as a 4-6-2-2. However, Gresley himself decreed that the engine was a 4-6-4. *British Rail*

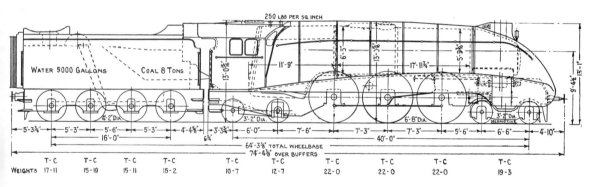

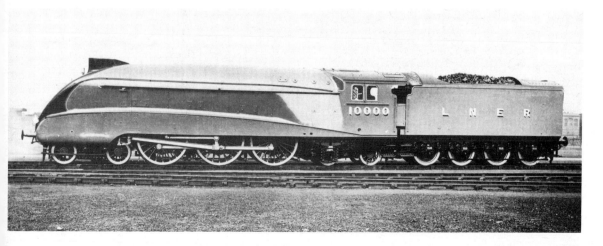

much liked by the drivers. The firemen, let it be said, were less enthusiastic about the larger grate area!

No 10000 had a limited route availability and it spent all its remaining years working on East Coast main line expresses from Kings Cross. During the war it had the side valances removed from ahead of the cylinders, and over the coupled wheels, in similar fashion to the Class A4 Pacifics. It was finally withdrawn from service in June 1959 and unfortunately was not a candidate for preservation.

The basic dimensions of the rebuilt engine were as follows:

Heating surface, tubes
  Larger and small: 2,361.0sq ft
  Firebox: 237.0sq ft

Total (evaporative): 2,598.0sq ft
Superheater: 750.0sq ft
  Combined heating surfaces: 3,585.0sq ft
  Superheater elements: 43
Grate area: 50.0sq ft
Tractive effort (at 85 per cent BP): 41,435lb

Below: Class W1 4-6-4 No 10000 is seen at Newark, at the head of a Leeds-Kings Cross express, in prewar days. *T. G. Hepburn*

Bottom: The Class W1 4-6-4 attracts the attention of a passenger in an adjacent train as it overtakes it and heads out of York with a through train from South Shields to Kings Cross on 5 July 1952. The engine is in its final livery of Brunswick green with orange and black lining. *R. K. Evans*

SECTION 23

**2-6-0 (3-cyl) LNER Class K4,
BR Power Class 5P6F
Mixed-Traffic Engines
Introduced: 1937
Total: 5**

A feature of Sir Nigel Gresley's locomotive policy for the LNER was his willingness to design locomotives for specific routes, and not adhere to a rigid standardisation policy. Thus, when more powerful locomotives were required for the tough West Highland line, he at first considered the use of an eight-coupled design. This however was not acceptable to the Civil Engineer as its weight and length would have been too great. Similarly, the Civil Engineer rejected the idea of using the existing 'K3' Class 2-6-0s.

Sir Nigel Gresley, having accepted the limitations imposed by the Civil Engineer, then set out to produce the most powerful Mogul that could be used over the route; with a good steaming boiler, small wheels for good adhesion and three cylinders. The 'K4' class, as it became known, had a shortened version of the 'B17' class boiler, standard 'K3' class cylinders and motion and 5ft 2in driving wheels. The boiler pressure was at first set to 180lb per sq in, producing a tractive effort of 32,940lb; later the pressure was raised to 200lb per sq in, and the tractive effort increased to 36,598lb (higher than a Class A4 Pacific). The engines were allowed to work loads of up to 300 tons over the West Highland, compared with the 220 tons maximum allowed for a single Class K2 2-6-0. Their small wheels restricted their maximum speed to around the mile-a-minute mark, on level stretches. A standard 3,500 gallon tender was attached.

The engines were built as follows:

| No 3441 | Darlington | 1937 |
| Nos 3442-3446 | Darlington | 1938/39 |

(In 1946 the class became Nos 1993-1998 respectively)

When first completed at Darlington, No 3441 was finished in black livery, but soon it and the rest of the class received full apple green passenger livery. They were popular engines and worked well on the West Highland when first delivered, but with the outbreak of war and a reduction in maintenance standards their day-to-day operation began to suffer, in common with the other Gresley three-cylinder classes.

As described in Appendix 2 Sir Nigel Gresley's successor, Mr Edward Thompson, selected one of the 'K4's, No 3445 *MacCailin Mor,* for rebuilding as a two-cylinder engine. This became, in effect, the prototype for the 'K1' class 2-6-0s.

Last of class withdrawn: (1961)
Example preserved: No 3442 (61994)

The basic dimensions of the class, as built, were as follows:

**Heating surface, tubes
  Large and small: 1,253.6sq ft
  Firebox: 168.0sq ft
Total (evaporative): 1,421.6sq ft
Superheater: 310.0sq ft
  Combined heating surfaces: 1,731.6sq ft
  Superheater elements: 24
Grate area: 27.5sq ft
Tractive effort (at 85 per cent BP): 32,939lb**

Below: Class K4 mixed-traffic three-cylinder 2-6-0, as first built, with 180lb per sq in boiler pressure.

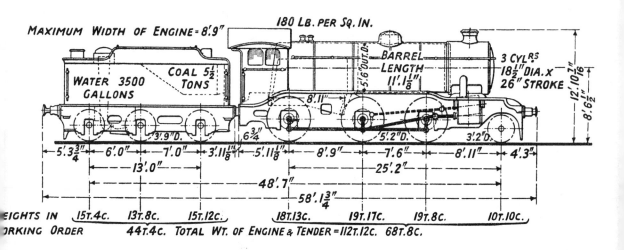

Top right: At the head of the 'Northern Belle' special tourist cruise train, Class K4 2-6-0 No 3446 *MacLeod of MacLeod* is seen here entering Crianlarich in 1938. Full apple green livery was applied to the class when new. The vacuum brake reservoir is visible on the tank top, at the rear of the tender. *A. B. MacLeod*

Centre right: Another view of *MacLeod of MacLeod,* by this time renumbered 1998, taken as the engine was leaving Crianlarich on the 6.00pm Glasgow Queen Street-Fortwilliam train one day in August 1946. *A. B. MacLeod*

Below: Taking the 'Road to the Isles' at Mallaig, in June 1951, is Class K4 2-6-0 No 61995 *Cameron of Lochiel,* on the down 10.25am Fort William-Mallaig train. The engine is in postwar LNER apple green livery, but has been renumbered into the BR series by the addition of 60000 to the number. Note the speedometer drive from rear coupled axle. *E. D. Bruton*

Above: Although still in the postwar LNER apple green, this Class K4, No 61998 *MacLeod of MacLeod,* had received both its new BR number and the full legend 'British Railways' on the tender sides by June 1950, when it was photographed arriving at Mallaig. The rolling stock is in a mixture of BR carmine red and cream and LNER teak livery. *W. J. V. Anderson*

Centre right: BR decided to paint the Class K4 2-6-0s in the standard lined black livery for mixed-traffic engines, as seen here on No 61993 *Loch Long,* photographed in June 1956. Front footsteps had been added to the engine, in rather crude fashion, and although the bracket was still carried, there was by then no drive to the speedometer from the rear coupled wheels. *D. Marriott*

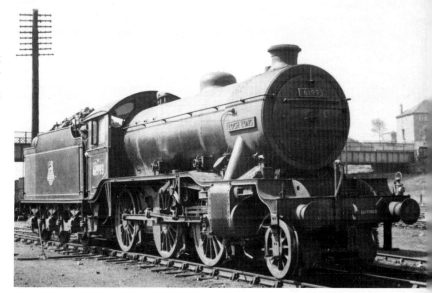

Bottom right: On the turntable at Fort William shed on 18 June 1960, Class K4 2-6-0 No 61995 *Cameron of Lochiel* is being prepared for the return leg of a special Stephenson Locomotive Society working. Smokebox numberplate with pale blue background, and nameplate with red background. No 61995 has elbow-shaped steampipes to the outside cylinders, similar to those on the Class VI 2-6-2Ts. *G. W. Morrison*

149

2-6-2 (3-cyl) LNER Class V4, BR Power Class 4MT Mixed-Traffic Engines
Introduced: 1941
Total: 2

The final design produced by Sir Nigel Gresley before his untimely death was a most attractive little 2-6-2, the Class V4, specifically intended as a powerful modern replacement for the many branch line and secondary duty engines of various classes, most of which were obsolescent and very uneconomical to maintain. In view of the nature of these duties, the new engine had to be kept as light as possible, and a new boiler was designed with a wide firebox and a working pressure of 250lb per sq in. Three cylinders were fitted and the coupled wheels were 5ft 8in. To keep weight down the boiler barrel was built from 2 per cent nickel steel, and there was extensive use of welding and fabricated parts, instead of the usual castings. The coupled axle loading was only 17 tons and this gave the class a very high route availability.

The introduction of this new and useful design took place at a most unfortunate time. World War 2 was in full spate, and there were shortages of materials for locomotive building. Also the work-shops were busy producing armaments and other supplies for the war effort, and so it was not until February 1941 that the prototype engine, No 3401 *Bantam Cock,* was completed at Doncaster, having been designed in 1939. A second engine No 3402 was completed the following month. This one had an all-steel welded firebox instead of copper as on No 3401 for comparative purposes, and it had a Nicholson thermic syphon.

After some initial trials on the GE Section, during which it proved a capable engine and a good steamer, No 3401 moved to Scotland, to be joined there by the second engine. They gained a good reputation for haulage and acceleration, but in the difficult conditions of the time, they proved to be expensive to maintain. They were also costly to build when compared to an equivalent mixed-traffic two-cylinder type. The greatly changed conditions in which the LNER had to operate from 1941 onwards could not have been foreseen by Sir Nigel Gresley when he first conceived the design in 1938, and Edward Thompson did not proceed with any further construction of the 'V4' class; introducing his new Class B1 4-6-0 instead.

Both engines were withdrawn in 1957, the last being No 3402
None preserved

The basic dimensions of the class were as follows:

Heating surface, tubes
   Large and small: 1,295.5sq ft
   Firebox: 151.6sq ft
Total (evaporative): 1,444.1sq ft
Superheater: 355.8sq ft
   Combined heating surfaces: 1,799.9sq ft
   Superheater elements: 22
Grate area: 28.5sq ft
Tractive effort (at 85 per cent BP): 27,420lb

Below: Class V4 lightweight three-cylinder mixed traffic 2-6-2 design.

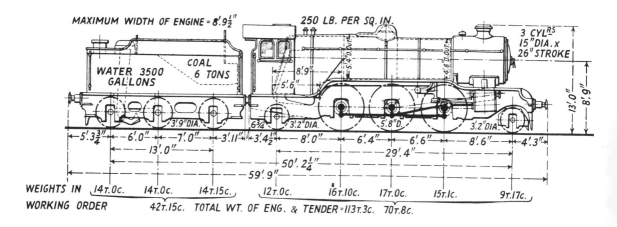

Below: Class V4 2-6-2 No 3401 *Bantam Cock* was sent to the GE Section for trials, when new, and is seen here near Cambridge on an express bound for Liverpool Street, hauling 14 coaches plus a six-wheeled brakevan; weighing over 450 tons tare. Note the GE style white headcode discs. *LPC*

Bottom: The second engine, not named but unofficially called *Bantam Hen;* No 3402 is seen here when brand new in full apple green livery but with a reminder of wartime in the form of the blackout tarpaulin between cab roof and tender top. This was Gresley's last design, and one which was once referred to as 'Rolls Royce engines to do a Ford car job'. It certainly had the style and elegance of the more expensive car! *British Rail*

Above: Standing on shed at Fort William in 1947, No 1700 *Bantam Cock* (it was renumbered in 1946) still carries the black livery and abbreviated tender initials of the wartime period. *Photomatic*

Centre right: Another view of No 1700 *Bantam Cock* in plain black livery, at the head of a through Glasgow-Fort William freight train, photographed near Crianlarich. *P. Ransome-Wallis*

Bottom right: Restored to postwar LNER apple green livery, but renumbered and lettered 'British Railways' on the tender, Class V4 2-6-2 No 61701 was photographed at Eastfield shed in June 1949. *H. C. Casserley*

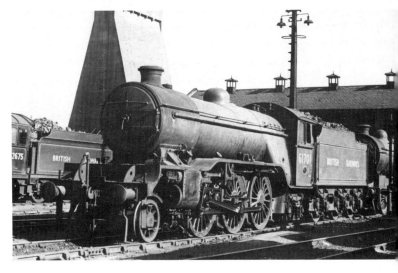

Appendices

1 Modifications to Existing Designs

One of Gresley's greatest attributes was his constant thirst for knowledge and improvement, a characteristic he shared with his Personal Assistant, O. V. S. Bulleid, and with his contemporary, the great French locomotive engineer, André Chapelon. Unlike some British CMEs, who viewed the products of their predecessors with obvious disdain, Gresley kept an open mind, and was quick to acknowledge the true merits of, for example, the engines produced by Robinson for the Great Central, and Holden and Hill for the Great Eastern. He took this acknowledgement a stage further, by building further examples of their engines for the LNER, and by rebuilding and improving others.

His work on the Ivatt Atlantics and the Holden 4-6-0s, making their performance sparkle as a result, has already been mentioned in the Introduction. He also applied some experimental gadgetry to some of them, and to other pre-Grouping types, in his quest for greater efficiency. Some of these applications were made whilst the drawing office was getting one or other of his new designs under way, and were obviously with a view to using the feedwater heater, or booster, or whatever it might be, on the new design. These 'guinea-pig' engines often suffered visually as a result! The illustrations in this Appendix depicts the main modifications and rebuilds undertaken by Gresley; there were of course countless smaller modifications made to individual locomotives.

Below: The idea of a booster, to give extra power to an engine when starting away from rest, or when climbing a steep gradient, had won popularity in North America, and Gresley gave serious study to its suitability in LNER operating conditions. He took a large superheated Ivatt Atlantic, No 4419, shortly after the Grouping in 1923 and fitted the trailing wheels with a small booster engine; providing an additional 8,500lb of tractive effort. Because the main frames had to be lengthened at the rear, a larger new side-window cab was fitted. Later the boiler mountings on No 4419 were cut down to permit running in Scotland. In 1925 his two large Mikados appeared, fitted with boosters as a result of experience with No 4419. Eventually No 4419 had the booster removed and ran out its days as an orthodox engine of its class, except that it retained the more commodious side-window cab. *LPC*

Above: In 1924, Large Atlantic No 4447 was modified to suit the NB loading gauge, with an altered cab and cut-down chimney and boiler mountings. No 4447 is seen here at York, in this condition. Note the raised inset to the lower portion of the cabside cutaway and the folding glass spectacle plate on cabside. *T. G. Hepburn*

Centre right: Two former NER three-cylinder Atlantics were equipped by Gresley with ACFI feedwater heaters in 1927. The ACFI system was popular on the Continent, in France especially, and the maker claimed that good economies in coal and water were achieved with engines so fitted. The mass of plumbing did nothing for the graceful looks of the two Atlantics, which were Nos 728 and 2206 of Class C7. *Ian Allan Library*

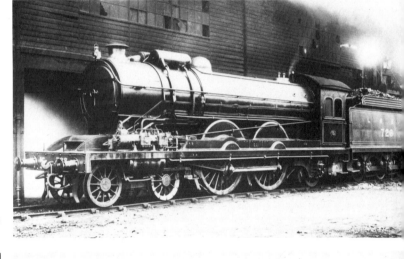

Bottom right: Gresley extended his ACFI feedwater heater experiments to some ex-GER 4-6-0s, and these gained the nickname of 'Hikers'. LNER Class B12 No 8517 is illustrated. Results with these ACFI applications were apparently promising enough for Gresley to extend them to two of his Pacifics. *LPC*

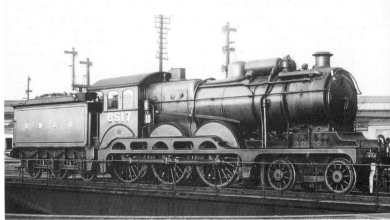

Top: Class C11 4-4-2 No 9903 *Cock o' the North,* a former NBR Reid Atlantic, was fitted in 1926 with a Worthington feedwater heater and pump, in place of the right-hand injector, a feature it retained until withdrawal. This engine was, incidentally, renamed *Aberdonian* in May 1934, so that its name could be used by Gresley for his new Class P2 2-8-2 No 2001. *Photomatic*

Above: Gresley's interest in the use of poppet valves instead of piston valves found its first practical application in 1927 on a Class B12 4-6-0 No 8516, as a result of which a batch of ten new 'B12s' were ordered from Beyer, Peacock, fitted with Lentz oscillating-cam gear. Experience with these then led Gresley to fit Caprotti valve gear to two of Robinson's ex GCR 'Lord Farringdon' class 4-6-0s, in 1929, with consequent improvement to their performance. No 6166 *Earl Haig* is illustrated here. *LPC*

Below: Another Robinson GCR design, his classic outside-cylinder 2-8-0 of Class 8K, introduced in 1911 (and manufactured during World War 1 in hundreds, for war service with the Railway Operating Division), was the subject of Nigel Gresley's attentions. Rather than build more boilers of Robinson's design, Gresley sought to use his own Class O2 2-8-0 boiler as a replacement. Two engines were rebuilt in 1929, Nos 6287 and 6371, and to carry the 'O2' boilers they had to have their frames lengthened, at the same time receiving a rather odd little cab with a single side window. Later rebuilds retained the original GCR style cab, and had a shortened version of the 'O2' boiler, thereby keeping the original frame length. A number of variations on this theme were produced by both Gresley and his successor, Thompson. *LPC*

Bottom: In 1931 Gresley converted the ex NER Class D 4-4-4Ts to 4-6-2Ts, to give them greater adhesion for service in the Tees-side area. (Prior to this he had ordered a batch of Robinson 4-6-2Ts specifically for this traffic). The rebuilt Raven tanks became LNER Class A8. No 9870 is seen at Darlington in ex-Works condition, in the plain postwar black livery, with unshaded Gill Sans lettering and numerals. *E. V. Fry*

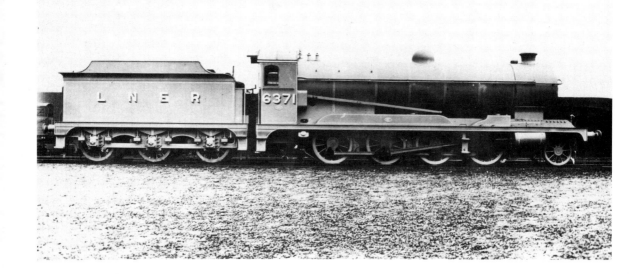

Above: A further experiment with booster engines took place in 1931, when Gresley selected two ex NER Atlantics, Class C7 Nos 727 and 2171, and fitted a four-wheeled bogie, articulated between engine and tender. This bogie carried the booster engine. He fitted larger boilers, of 200lb per sq in pressure, and the rebuilding included raised running plates and a side-window cab, and modified 4,125gal flush-sided tenders. As the tender also carried a bogie, the wheel arrangement of these engines was strictly speaking 4-4-4-4. *Photomatic*

Below: Gresley further improved some of the GE Section 4-6-0s and 4-4-0s by rebuilding them with new boilers and redesigned front ends (see also page 15). In the case of the 'Claud Hamilton' 4-4-0s, the original chassis was retained, with new piston valve cylinders. Classified D16/3, these engines were rebuilt at Stratford works in 1933/34, and demonstrated much improved performance. In BR days No 62571 is seen at Lowdham with a Nottingham-Lincoln train, on 21 March 1958. *J. P. Wilson*

Above: Other GE Section types to receive Gresley's attentions were the two 0-6-0 goods engine Classes, J18 and J19. All these received Gresley round-topped firebox boilers and a slight reduction in cylinder diameter, from 20in to 19in. Otherwise they remained as before, and the two classes were then grouped together and reclassified J19/2. Illustrated is No 64668 at the head of an up Class 'H' freight train near Bishops Stortford on 29 August 1952. *R. E. Vincent*

Centre right: In 1933 Gresley rebuilt an ex-NER Class C7 Atlantic with Lentz rotary cam-operated poppet valves, similar to those used on the Class D49/2 'Hunt' class 4-4-0s. This was No 732. Then in 1936 No 2212 (which had been the subject of an experiment using 'Uniflow' cylinders in NER days) was rebuilt to the same pattern, but using the improved Lentz gear with seven instead of five exhaust positions. Both were classified Class C7/2 No 2212 is illustrated at Gateshead shed in 1937, with Class A1 Pacific No 2576 *The White Knight* in the background, fitted with a feedwater heater. *P. Ransome-Wallis*

Bottom right: The four-cylinder simple Atlantic No 279 (see page 10) was again rebuilt by Gresley in 1936, as a two-cylinder engine with outside Walschaerts valve gear. In this form it was probably the most 'modern' looking engine in the class. The cylinders were of the 'K2' pattern with some refinements, and a new, larger cab was fitted. No 3279 is seen at the head of a Grimsby-Kings Cross working, soon after rebuilding. *T. G. Hepburn*

Above: One ex-NER Class R (LNER Class D20) 4-4-0 was rebuilt with long-travel valves, in 1936. The running plate was raised over the driving wheels, but the original boiler, chimney and dome were retained. This was No 2020, and the engine is seen here in BR days, as No 62349, double-heading with an Ivatt Class 4 2-6-0, on a lengthy express from the LMR Central Division to Filey, Bridlington and Scarborough, in July 1955. *P. J. Lynch*

Below: Another former NER design to receive Gresley's attentions was the Class S3 (LNER 'B16') three-cylinder mixed traffic 4-6-0. Gresley selected No 2364 and in 1938 fitted new cylinders, Walschaerts valve gear for the outside cylinders and his derived gear for the inside cylinder. The rebuild was Classified B16/2, and six further examples followed. Later, Edward Thompson was to rebuild further engines of the class, but with independent sets of gear for each cylinder. No 61457 was photographed near Chaloner's Whin, York, in BR days. *Eric Treacy*

2 Subsequent Rebuilds of Gresley Locomotives

At the time when Edward Thompson was appointed to the post of Chief Mechanical Engineer of the LNER on 28 April 1941, following the death of Sir Nigel Gresley, the locomotive stock of the company was being extremely hard pressed to serve the war effort, and both staff and materials shortages were severe indeed. The sophisticated three-cylinder Gresley engines, with their derived valve gear were clearly suffering under these poor conditions, and it was part of Thompson's philosophy to try and simplify locomotive design, to make maintenance cheaper, easier and quicker.

Thompson instituted some staff changes within the CME's department, and then set about putting his ideas into practical form; in so doing arousing some hostility and resentment, let it be said. It was Thompson, incidentally, who removed the valances from the streamlined Gresley engines, to make maintenance easier. But soon more radical changes were to come, particularly in respect of valve gear design. Thompson had never admired the Gresley conjugated valve gear for the three-cylinder engines, but whilst maintenance was good this dislike was not sufficient grounds for radical redesign. Under wartime conditions, however, a stronger case for rethinking valve gear design existed. Thompson was able to convince the LNER Directors that a locomotive rebuilding and standardisation programme should be instituted. Some of the rebuilds were to be from old Robinson Great Central Railway engines and were undertaken to provide much needed freight and shunting locomo-tives, but others were rebuilds of much newer Gresley designs, including his pioneer Class A1 Pacific, his 'P2' 2-8-2s and certain other types; as depicted in the illustrations that follow.

Thompson also cancelled an outstanding order for 10 Class V4 lightweight three cylinder 2-6-2s, and introduced instead his own two cylinder Class B1 mixed-traffic 4-6-0 design, and he ordered that the last four of a batch of Gresley Class V2 2-6-2s should be redesigned and completed as Pacifics. Thus the final locomotives of Gresley design were never completed as ordered, such was the speed of the winds of change in LNER locomotive policy after the great man's death. What followed is, of course, another story.

Below: One locomotive of the Class D49 4-4-0s was altered by Thompson from a three-cylinder to a two-cylinder engine in 1942, and then reclassified 'D49/2'. The original rotary cam valve gear was replaced by a pair of inside cylinders with Stephenson motion and piston valves. Although four more rebuilds were ordered, the performance of No 365 *The Morpeth* (seen here in wartime black livery) was so disappointing that the order was cancelled in 1948. No 365 ran in this form until November 1952, when it was withdrawn following collision damage. *Ian Allan Library*

Below: Thompson's aim, to introduce a greater degree of standardisation and simplicity into the LNER locomotive fleet, was reflected in his proposal for a mixed-traffic Pacific, based upon the 'A4' but without streamlining and with a standard tender. This locomotive was to replace the 'P1', 'P2' and 'V2' classes, as well as taking over the heavier duties performed by the 'B7', 'B16' and 'K3' classes. He chose to rebuild the Gresley Class P2 Mikados as the first examples of these Pacifics, to his design, using their known weaknesses in the motion and bearings as a case for rebuilding. He fitted three independent sets of valve motion, with the middle cylinder set well forward; all three cylinders had connecting rods of equal length. A Kylchap double blastpipe with stovepipe-style chimney was fitted, with small smoke deflector wings (as carried by the 'A3' *Humorist* at one stage). All six engines were rebuilt as Class A2, in 1943-44 at Doncaster; retaining their names. No 502 *Earl Marischal* is seen here in postwar apple green livery. *P. Ransome-Wallis*

Bottom: Thompson decided to build four Class A2/1 Pacifics at Darlington in 1944 instead of the final four engines of the Gresley Class V2 2-6-2 which had actually been ordered. The design used as much of the 'V2' parts as possible but the front end was based upon the design produced for the rebuilding of the Class P2s as Pacifics. The six-wheeled standard tenders intended for the 'V2s' were retained. It could be said that the front half of the engine was Thompson's and the rear half was Gresley's! Illustrated is the first one, No 3696, in shop grey livery. Nos 3696-3699 became Nos 507-510 in 1946. They were named in the period 1946-48, with No 3696 (507) becoming *Highland Chieftain.* Later they ran with eight-wheeled tenders. *British Rail*

Above: When Class B17 4-6-0 No 2871 fell due for heavy repairs, Thompson decided to rebuild the engine using parts of his standard pattern. this included a 'B1' type boiler, two new outside cylinders (eliminating the third cylinder), a new driving axle and a new bogie. Reclassified 'B2', 10 locomotives were dealt with in this fashion: Nos (1946 renumbering) 1603/7/14-17/32/9/44/71. Tenders of NER origin were fitted. No 1603 *Framlingham* in postwar plain black livery with unshaded Gill Sans lettering is seen here at Colchester on a Liverpool Street-Clacton express in June 1947. *Ian Allan Library*

Below: A solitary rebuild was the Class K5 2-6-0 No 1863, which Thompson produced from a Gresley Class K3 three-cylinder engine. This locomotive had two outside cylinders with Walschaerts valve gear (having parts in common with Thompson's own 'B1', 'L1' and 'O1' classes), and a boiler of 225lb per sq in. A new design of pony truck replaced the Gresley double swing-link truck, and a new driving axle was provided. This fairly costly rebuild had a reputation for becoming rough very soon after an overhaul and it is perhaps significant that Thompson chose another Gresley 2-6-0, the Class K4, as the basis for his own standard mixed-traffic Mogul. *E. R. Wethersett*

Top: As a basis for his future medium power range standard mixed-traffic and goods engine, Thompson selected a Class K4 Gresley three-cylinder 2-6-0, *MacCailin Mor* and rebuilt it using as many of his standard parts as possible, including new cylinders and two sets of outside Walschaerts valve gear. This engine proved to be considerably more successful in service than his 'K5' rebuild, and Thompson's successor introduced 70 locomotives of 'K1' design from 1949 onward, largely based upon this rebuild. Classified K1, No 3445 is seen here in wartime black livery, when just rebuilt in 1945. *Ian Allan Library*

Above: The most controversial of all the Thompson rebuilds was undoubtedly the Pacific No 4470 *Great Northern.* This had remained a Class A1 (later A10) throughout its life and Thompson selected it for a more drastic conversion than that of becoming an 'A3'; as had

been anticipated. This was, of course, Gresley's pioneer Pacific locomotive and was held in great esteem by many railwaymen and enthusiasts. Although officially described as a rebuild, the original engine was actually dismantled and what emerged from Doncaster was virtually a completely new machine, with some remarkably ugly features which were intended to ease maintenance. With three separate cylinders and 6ft 8in coupled wheels, the rebuild was the prototype for the postwar express passenger Pacifics by Thompson and Peppercorn. Painted in GER deep ultramarine blue livery, with red lining. No 4470 *Great Northern* is seen here in September 1945, when just completed. Features of interest included the provision of electric lighting, a rocking grate, raised running plates over the coupled wheels and a short side sheet to the cab (later modified to more normal dimensions). Only the tender served as a reminder of the more graceful days of Sir Nigel Gresley's locomotives for the LNER. *British Rail*

3 Steam and Diesel Railcars

By the mid-1920s the steady growth of road transport, which had begun after the end of World War 1, was seriously threatening the survival of some rural and local train services on the LNER. The private car, in particular, was taking rural traffic away and to counter this the railway company sought a method of motive power which was cheap to operate, and attractive to travel in. The answer was found in a modern development of the steam railmotor, using a high-speed Sentinel geared engine powered by a high-pressure water-tube boiler. Horsepower was a nominal 100-125hp. The locomotive portion was carried on a four-wheel bogie with a chain drive; later this was changed to a geared drive. The power bogie was articulated to a lightweight coach body, which had another bogie at the rear end. The carriage body enclosed the engine portion and the coal and water space (except on the Clayton railcars, where the coal bunker was oddly placed outside).

The LNER tested a Sentinel-Cammell railcar in Yorkshire in 1924, and then bought two similar cars the following year. These were considered successful and two more followed in 1927; then an order for 20 more was placed and delivered in 1928. By 1930 the LNER had a fleet of nearly 90 steam railcars. The original livery was immitation teak, as on the wooden carriages (the railcar bodies were metal), later this was changed to red and cream, and finally to apple green and cream. The railcars were classed as follows (the numbers were in the LNER carriage list):

Below: Sentinel-Cammell two-cylinder chain-driven steam railcar No 26 *Tally-ho* built in 1928, and classified Type F. *Author's Collection*

Sentinel-Cammell two-cylinder chain-driven cars Types D, E and F.

No 43306	—	1925
No 43307	—	1925
No 21	*Valliant*	1927
No 22	*Brilliant*	1927
No 26	*Tally-Ho*	1928
No 29	*Rockingham*	1928
No 210	*High Flyer*	1928
No 212	*Eclipse*	1928
No 220	*Water Witch*	1928
No 225	*True Blue*	1928
No 226	*Ebor*	1928
No 237	*Rodney*	1928
No 238	*Yorkshire Hussar*	1928
No 244	*True Briton*	1928
No 250	*Rob Roy*	1928
No 253	*Red Rover*	1928
No 254	*Phoenix*	1928
No 255	*Perseverance*	1928
No 263	*North Star*	1928
No 265	*Neptune*	1928
No 267	*Liberty*	1928
No 272	*Hero*	1928
No 273	*Travalgar*	1928
No 283	*Teazle*	1928

Nos 43306/7 were Nos 12E and 13E until 1931/2 respectively)

Clayton geared steam railcars. Types A, B & C.

No 2121	*Pilot*	1927
No 285	*Rapid*	1928
No 287	*Royal Sailor*	1928
No 289	*Wellington*	1928
No 296	*Wonder*	1928
No 2101	*Union*	1928
No 2110	*Comet*	1928
No 2120	*Chevy Chase*	1928
No 2122	*Railway*	1928

| No 2130 | *Bang Up* | 1928 |
| No 61999 | *Transit* | 1928 |

(No 2120 became No 42, then in 1934 it became No 43302. No 2122 became No 43, then in 1935 it became No 43303. No 2130 became No 44, then in 1934 it became No 43304).

All the Clayton cars were withdrawn from service by 1937.

Below: Clayton steam railcar No 289 *Wellington* photographed at Newcastle Central in August 1933. This was one of the batch delivered in 1928. The Clayton cars had one end of the passenger carriage resting on a four-wheel coupled power unit, and the coal bunker was rather oddly sited outside the coach and over the bogie; somewhat restricting the driver's forward vision. *Photomatic*

Sentinel two-cylinder gear-driven car. Type G.

| No 2135 | *Integrity* | 1928 |

Sentinel six-cylinder gear-driven cars. Type H.

No 35	*Nettle*	1928
No 2133	*Cleveland*	1928
No 2136	*Hope*	1928
No 2139	*Hark Forward*	1928
No 2140	*Eagle*	1928
No 2144	*Traveller*	1928
No 2145	*Ruby*	1928
No 2147	*Woodpecker*	1928
No 2151	*Umpire*	1928
No 2152	*Courrier*	1928
No 31	*Flower of Yarrow*	1928
No 43301	*Commerce*	1928
No 51908	*Expedition*	1928

Right: Sentinel two-cylinder gear driven steam railcar No 2135 *Integrity*, built in 1928 and classified as Type G. In general layout this was similar to the earlier chain-driven railcars but it had the engine mounted within a completely rigid body, driving a flexible bogie through gears, via a universal joint and cardan shaft. The engine was of 100hp. Only No 2135 featured a two-cylinder engine and gear drive; all subsequent railcars were fitted with an improved 6-cylinder type. *Integrity* is seen here leaving Newcastle Central in August 1932. *Photomatic*

No 51909	Waterloo	1929
No 32	Fair Maid	1929
No 33	Highland Chieftain	1929
No 34	Tweedside	1929
No 36	Royal Eagle	1929
No 37	Clydesdale	1929
No 38	Pearl	1929
No 39	Protector	1929
No 310	Prince Regent	1929
No 31073	Quicksilver	1929
No 312	Retaliator	1929
No 51912	Rising Sun	1929
No 51913	Rival	1929
No 51914	Royal Forrester	1929
No 2198	Times	1929
No 2200	Surprise	1929
No 2217	Royal Charlotte	1929
No 2218	Telegraph	1929
No 2219	New Fly	1929
No 2231	Swift	1929
No 2232	Alexander	1929
No 2235	Britannia	1929
No 2236	British Queen	1929
No 2238	Celerity	1929
No 2242	Cornwallis	1929
No 2245	Criterion	1929
No 2257	Defiance	1929
No 2261	Diligence	1929
No 2267	Recovery	1929
No 2268	Emerald	1929
No 2270	Independent	1929
No 2271	Industry	1929
No 2276	North Briton	1930
No 2279	Norfolk	1930
No 313	Banks of Don	1931
No 314	Queen of Beauty	1931

(No 35 was No 2133 for a short period when new. No 43301 was originally No 45. No 33 was No 71 for a month in 1931. No 31073 was originally No 311, and No 2276 ran as No 31070 from 1931-1933).

A car of similar design, which ran on the Axholme Joint Railway (built 1930) was taken over from the LMSR in November 1933 and became LNER No 51915.

Sentinel twin-engine 200hp railcars. Type Ha
These cars were specially built with two engines, for use on exceptionally hilly routes.

No 2281	Old John Bull	1930
No 2283	Old Blue	1930
No 220	Defence	1932
No 246	Royal Sovereign	1932
No 248	Tantivy	1932

Sentinel two-car articulated unit. Type J.

No 2291	Phenomena	1930

The seating in the various types of railcar varied from only 44 on the Clayton car *Bang Up* to an

Below: Six-cylinder Sentinel gear driven Type H railcar No 2271 *Industry,* built in 1929. This was the standard LNER steam railcar design with accommodation for 59 passengers. To cope with extra loads a four-wheeled trailer car could be hauled, as seen in this photograph taken near Darlington in July 1934, with the railcar working a Richmond branch train. *Photomatic*

average of 59 in the single cars, and a total of 132 in the two-car articulated unit. Eight lightweight four-wheel trailer cars were built in 1929, but were not a great success. The steam railcars were not powerful enough to haul a standard passenger bogie carriage, and their limited seating capacity was a problem to the operators. All the names they carried were those of old road stage coaches. The last steam railcar was scrapped in 1948.

Of the four diesel railcars which ran on the LNER during the Gresley era, three were of basically similar design and were built by Armstrong Whitworth, with a 250hp diesel-electric power unit. These were as follows:

No 25	Tyneside Venturer	1931
No 224	Lady Hamilton	1934
No 232	Northumbrian	1934

The fourth diesel railcar was a lightweight streamlined design with a 95hp engine; this was numbered 294 and was built in 1933. It did not carry a name.

Top: Armstrong-Whitworth diesel-electric railcar No 232 *Northumbrian,* seen at York in August 1935, on a Harrogate train. This was one of three similar railcars, the first of which was tried out on the LNER in 1931, in the Newcastle area. Taken into stock in 1934 it became No 25 *Tyneside Venturer* and the same year saw two more, No 224 *Lady Hamilton* and the one illustrated here, also enter service. A 250hp engine was fitted and they were capable of towing a standard coach as a trailer. The livery was a very attractive deep blue and cream. *Photomatic*

Above: The fourth diesel railcar to be used by the LNER was a streamlined vehicle with a 95hp engine. No 294 (which was not given a name) was of a lightweight design which meant that it was not equipped to haul trailers of any description. It was built by Armstrong-Whitworth in 1933 and is seen here at Newcastle Central in 1934. *Photomatic*

The diesel railcars were not very successful in traffic, and by 1939 all were withdrawn; being stored and not actually broken up until after the end of World War 2.

4 Electric Locomotives

In 1936 the LNER decided to electrify the former GCR route across the Pennines, from Sheffield to Manchester, using the 1,500V dc overhead system. This route carried particularly heavy coal traffic, and included some considerable gradients. A prototype electric locomotive was produced by Gresley ahead of completion of the electrification, in 1941. The war, and the need to build a new tunnel at Woodhead, delayed completion of the scheme until 1954. Meanwhile the prototype locomotive, which had been stored during the war, was sent to the Netherlands Railways for evaluation.

The locomotive, originally numbered 6701, was a Bo + Bo, with the buffer beams integral with the bogie frames, which were coupled at their inner ends by an articulated joint and transmitted the tractive effort; the maximum rail horsepower was 3,300 and the engine weighed 87 tons. In 1950-53 a further 56 locomotives of similar design were built by British Railways, and a number were still in service at the beginning of 1980, although BR had announced its intention to close the route which had been freight only since 1970. The locomotives as built were equipped with regenerative braking, plus an air brake for the locomotive itself and an exhauster for vacuum-braked trains. In the late 1960s a number were fitted with larger exhausters to operate air brakes on the locomotive and its train, but the compressors were retained for working vacuum-braked stock; provision was made at the same time for multiple-unit working in pairs. When further locomotives were fitted with larger compressors and multiple-unit equipment in 1979, their exhausters were removed at the same time.

Right: To aid postwar recovery, and because it was surplus to LNER requirements (pending completion of the Manchester-Sheffield-Wath electrification), No 6000, as it later became, was sent to Holland for use on the Netherlands Railway system. In service it proved powerful, but extremely poor riding and some modification to the bogie design proved necessary. In this picture, taken at Eindehoven in September 1947, the locomotive had just taken over a 1050 ton coal train from an ex-War Department Riddles 2-10-0. Note the extended chimney and large headlights on the Riddles engine. Dutch railwaymen nicknamed the electric locomotive *Tommy,* and it carried nameplates to this effect when it returned to Britain. *Ian Allan Library*

Below right: British Rail Class 76 Bo+Bo 1500V dc electric No 76.050, in rail blue livery with yellow ends, at the head of a westbound coal train near Dinting in June 1974. The production version of the prewar Gresley design was delivered to the Eastern Region from 1950 onwards, and apart from some bogie modifications the 56 locomotives closely resembled the prototype introduced some 10 years previously. The first BR livery was lined black and they were numbered in the 26000 series, later they were Brunswick green, then 'electric' blue and finally rail blue. Their riding qualities were so poor that they were not normally used for fast passenger work, a larger Co-Co design being introduced by BR to meet this need instead. *Brian Morrison*

Right: Sir Nigel Gresley's prototype 1500V dc Bo+Bo electric locomotive, with Metropoliton-Vickers power equipment, seen on a proving trial over the Manchester-Altrincham line in 1941. World War 2 delayed the introduction of the Manchester-Sheffield-Wath electrification for which the design was intended, and in fact this did not reach completion until 1954. No 6701 was painted in apple green livery with black and white lining out, when new. Note the brass worksplate prominently displayed on the front of the locomotive, also the special daytime headcode discs placed over the electric headlights. The bufferbeam was integral with the bogie, and not attached to the main superstructure. *English Electric/AEI*

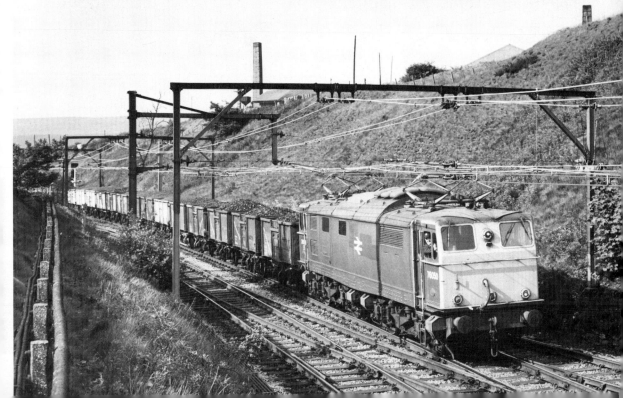

5 Named Locomotives

Showing all named Gresley locomotives taken over by British Railways, on 1 January 1948, and Gresley locomotives modified by Edward Thompson. The 1946 LNER numbers are given. All locomotives had 60000 added to their existing running numbers by BR, although for a while early in 1948, some locomotives carried the prefix E to their LNER numbers.

For ease of reference the original LNER number is shown before the 1946-47 BR number. Where a locomotive was rebuilt by Thompson it is shown with earlier Gresley numbers first. Locomotives renamed by the LNER or during nationalisation have the date of renaming or BR naming shown in brackets.

STEAM LOCOMOTIVES

4-6-2 Classes A1 (later A10) and A3
(see Sections 9 and 15)

2500	35	Windsor Lad
2501	36	Colombo
2502	37	Hyperion
2503	38	Firdaussi
2504	39	Sandwich
2505	40	Cameronian
2506	41	Salmon Trout
2507	42	Singapore
2508	43	Brown Jack
2543	44	Melton
2544	45	Lemberg
2545	46	Diamond Jubilee
2546	47	Donovan
2547	48	Doncaster
2548	49	Galtee More
2549	50	Persimmon
2550	51	Blink Bonny
2551	52	Prince Palatine
2552	53	Sansovino
2553	54	Manna
		(11/26) Prince of Wales
2554	55	Woolwinder
2555	56	Centenary
2556	57	Ormonde
2557	58	Blair Athol
2558	59	Tracery
2559	60	The Tetrarch
2560	61	Pretty Polly
2561	62	Minoru
2562	63	Isinglass
2563	64	William Whitelaw (8/41) Tagalie
2564	65	Knight of the Thistle
		(12/32) Knight of Thistle
2565	66	Merry Hampton
2566	67	Ladas

2567	68	Sir Visto
2568	69	Sceptre
2569	70	Gladiateur
2570	71	Tranquil
2571	72	Sunstar
2572	73	St Gatien
2573	74	Harvester
2574	75	St Frusquin
2575	76	Galopin
2576	77	The White Knight
2577	78	Night Hawk
2578	79	Bayardo
2579	80	Dick Turpin
2580	81	Shotover
2581	82	Neil Gow
2582	83	Sir Hugo
2595	84	Trigo
2596	85	Manna
2597	86	Gainsborough
2598	87	Blenheim
2599	88	Book Law
2743	89	Felstead
2744	90	Grand Parade
2745	91	Captain Cuttle
2746	92	Fairway
2747	93	Coronach
2748	94	Colorado
2749	95	Flamingo
2750	96	Papyrus
2751	97	Humorist
2752	98	Spion Kop
2795	99	Call Boy
2796	100	Spearmint
2797	101	Cicero
4471	102	Sir Frederick Banbury
4472	103	Flying Scotsman
4473	104	Solario
4474	105	Victor Wild
4475	106	Flying Fox
4476	107	Royal Lancer
4477	108	Gay Crusader
4478	109	Hermit
4479	100	Robert the Devil
4480	111	Enterprise
4481	112	St Simon
4470	113*	Great Northern

4-6-2 Class A4 *(see Section 20)*

4500	1	Garganey
		(3/39) Sir Ronald Matthews
4499	2	Pochard
		(4/39) Sir Murrough Wilson
4494	3	Osprey
		(10/42) Andrew K. McCosh
4462	4	Great Snipe
		(7/41) William Whitelaw

*Later rebuilt to Class A1/1 by Thompson.

170

4901	5	Capercaillie		4467	21	Wild Swan
		(9/42) Charles H. Newton		4468	22	Mallard
		(6/43) Sir Charles Newton		4469	–	Gadwall
4466	6	Herring Gull				(3/39) Sir Ralph Wedgwood
		(1/44) Sir Ralph Wedgwood		4482	23	Golden Eagle
4498	7	Sir Nigel Gresley		4483	24	Kingfisher
4496	8	Golden Shuttle		4484	25	Falcon
		(9/54) Dwight D. Eisenhower		4485	26	Kestrel
4488	9	Union of South Africa				(11/47) Miles Beevor
4489	10	Woodcock		4486	27	Merlin
		(6/37) Dominion of Canada		4487	28	Sea Eagle
4490	11	Empire of India				(10/47) Walter K. Whigham
4491	12	Commonwealth of Australia		4493	29	Woodcock
4492	13	Dominion of New Zealand		4495	30	Great Snipe
2509	14	Silver Link				(9/37) Golden Fleece
2510	15	Quicksilver		4497	31	Golden Plover
2511	16	Silver King		4900	32	Gannet
2512	17	Silver Fox		4902	33	Seagull
4463	18	Sparrow Hawk		4903	34	Peregrine
4464	19	Bittern				(3/48) Lord Faringdon
4465	20	Guillemot				

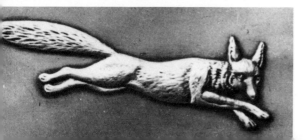

Above: Nameplate of Class A4 Pacific No 60007 *Sir Nigel Gresley,* as carried after the engine had been preserved and restored to garter blue livery. *Eric Treacy*

Top left: Stainless steel relief Gill Sans numerals, and crest on plate, attached to cabside of Class A4 Pacific No 4490 *Empire of India. Photomatic*

Centre left: Painted name, in silver with dark blue shading as first applied to Class A4 Pacific No 2510, in the centre of the boiler casing; later replaced by cast brass nameplates placed alongside the smokebox. *Photomatic*

Bottom left: The stainless steel replica of a flying fox (or fox on the run) which was carried on the boiler casing of Class A4 Pacific *Silver Fox* (originally No 2512; finally BR No 60017). This was made, and presented to the LNER, by the United Steel Companies, one of whose constituents was Samuel Fox & Co. *Photomatic*

4-6-0 Class B17 (see Section 16)

2800	1600	Sandringham
2801	1601	Holkham
*2802	1602	Walsingham
2803	1603	Framlingham
2804	1604	Elveden
2805	1605	Burnham Thorpe
		(4/38) Lincolnshire Regiment
2806	1606	Audley End
*2807	1607	Blickling
2808	1608	Gunton
2809	1609	Quidenham
2810	1610	Honingham Hall
2811	1611	Raynham Hall
2812	1612	Houghton Hall
2813	1613	Woodbastwick Hall
*2814	1614	Castle Hedingham
*2815	1615	Culford Hall
*2816	1616	Fallodon
*2817	1617	Ford Castle
2818	1618	Wynyard Park
2819	1619	Welbeck Abbey
2820	1620	Clumber
2821	1621	Hatfield House
2822	1622	Alnwick Castle
2823	1623	Lambton Castle
2824	1624	Lumley Castle
2825	1625	Raby Castle
2826	1626	Brancepeth Castle
2827	1627	Aske Hall
2828	1628	Harewood House
2829	1629	Naworth Castle
2830	1630	Thoresby Park
		(1/38) Tottenham Hotspur
2831	1631	Serlby Hall
*2832	1632	Belvoir Castle
		(10/58) Royal Sovereign
2833	1633	Kimbolton Castle
2834	1634	Hinchingbrooke
2835	1635	Milton
2836	1636	Harlaxton Manor
2837	1637	Thorpe Hall
2838	1638	Melton Hall
*2839	1639	Rendlesham Hall
		(1/38) Norwich City
2840	1640	Somerleyton Hall
2841	1641	Gayton Hall
2842	1642	Kilverstone Hall
2843	1643	Champion Lodge
*2844	1644	Earlham Hall
2845	1645	The Suffolk Regiment
2846	1646	Gilwell Park
2847	1647	Helmingham Hall
2848	1648	Arsenal
2849	1649	Sheffield United
2850	1650	Grimsby Town
2851	1651	Derby County
2852	1652	Darlington
2853	1653	Huddersfield Town
2854	1654	Sunderland
2855	1655	Middlesbrough
2856	1656	Leeds United
2857	1657	Doncaster Rovers
2858	1658	Newcastle United
		(6/36) The Essex Regiment
2859	1659	Norwich City
		(9/37) East Anglian
2860	1660	Hull City
2861	1661	Sheffield Wednesday
2862	1662	Manchester United
2863	1663	Everton
2864	1664	Liverpool
2865	1665	Leicester City
2866	1666	Nottingham Forest
2867	1667	Bradford
2868	1668	Bradford City
2869	1669	Barnsley
2870	1670	Manchester City
		(5/37) Tottenham Hotspur
		(9/37) City of London
*2871	1671	Manchester City
		(4/46) Royal Sovereign
2872	1672	West Ham United

4-4-0 Class D49 (see Section 14)

234	2700	Yorkshire
251	2701	Derbyshire
253	2702	Oxfordshire
256	2703	Hertfordshire
264	2704	Stirlingshire
265	2705	Lanarkshire
266	2706	Forfarshire
236	2707	Lancashire
270	2708	Argyllshire
277	2709	Berwickshire
245	2710	Lincolnshire
281	2711	Dumbartonshire
246	2712	Morayshire
249	2713	Aberdeenshire
250	2714	Perthshire
306	2715	Roxburghshire
307	2716	Kincardineshire
309	2717	Banffshire
310	2718	Kinross-shire
311	2719	Peebles-shire
318	2720	Cambridgeshire
320	2721	Warwickshire
322	2722	Huntingdonshire
327	2723	Nottinghamshire
335	2724	Bedfordshire
329	2725	Inverness-shire
352	2726	Leicestershire
		(6/32) The Meynell
336	2727	Buckinghamshire
		(5/32) The Quorn
2753	2728	Cheshire

*Rebuilt by Thompson to Class B2.

2754	2729	*Rutlandshire*
2755	2730	*Berkshire*
2756	2731	*Selkirkshire*
2757	2732	*Dumfries-shire*
2758	2733	*Northumberland*
2759	2734	*Cumberland*
2760	2735	*Westmorland*
201	2736	*The Bramham Moor*
211	2737	*The York and Ainsty*
220	2738	*The Zetland*
232	2739	*The Badsworth*
235	2740	*The Bedale*
247	2741	*The Blankney*
255	2742	*The Braes of Derwent*
269	2743	*The Cleveland*
273	2744	*The Holderness*
282	2745	*The Hurworth*
283	2746	*The Middleton*
288	2747	*The Percy*
292	2748	*The Southwold*
297	2749	*The Cottesmore*
298	2750	*The Pytchley*
205	2751	*The Albrighton*
214	2752	*The Atherstone*
217	2753	*The Belvoir*
222	2754	*The Berkeley*
226	2755	*The Bilsdale*
230	2756	*The Brocklesby*
238	2757	*The Burton*
258	2758	*The Cattistock*
274	2759	*The Craven*
279	2760	*The Cotswold*
353	2761	*The Derwent*
357	2762	*The Fernie*
359	2763	*The Fitzwilliam*
361	2764	*The Garth*
362	2765	*The Goathland*
363	2766	*The Grafton*
364	2767	*The Grove*
365	2768*	*The Morpeth*
366	2769	*The Oakley*
368	2770	*The Puckeridge*
370	2771	*The Rufford*
374	2772	*The Sinnington*
375	2773	*The South Durham*
376	2774	*The Staintondale*
377	2775	*The Tynedale*

2-6-0 Class K2 (see Section 4)

4674	1764	*Loch Arkaig*
4682	1772	*Loch Lochy*
4684	1774	*Loch Garry*
4685	1775	*Loch Treig*
4691	1781	*Loch Morar*
4692	1782	*Loch Eil*
4693	1783	*Loch Sheil*
4697	1787	*Loch Quoich*

*Later rebuilt to Class D49/4.

4698	1788	*Loch Rannoch*
4699	1789	*Loch Laidon*
4700	1790	*Loch Lomond*
4701	1791	*Loch Laggan*
4704	1794	*Loch Oich*

2-6-0 Class K4 (see Section 23)

3441	1993	*Loch Long*
3442	1994	*MacCailein Mór*
		(7/38) The Great Marquess
3443	1995	*Cameron of Lochiel*
3444	1996	*Lord of the Isles*
3445	1997†	*MacCailin Mór*
3446	1998	*Lord of Dunvegan*
		(3/39) MacLeod of MacLeod

2-8-2 Class P2* (see Section 19)

2001	501	*Cock o' the North*
2002	502	*Earl Marischal*
2003	503	*Lord President*
2004	504	*Mons Meg*
2005	505	*Thane of Fife*
2006	506	*Wolf of Badenoch*

2-6-2 Class V2 (see Section 21)

4771	800	*Green Arrow*
4780	809	*The Snapper*
		The East Yorkshire Regiment–
		The Duke of York's Own
4806	835	*The Green Howard*
		Alexandra, Princess of Wales's
		Own Yorkshire Regiment
4818	847	*St. Peter's School*
		York A.D. 627
4831	860	*Durham School*
4843	872	*King's Own Yorkshire Light Infantry*
4844	873	*Coldstreamer*
	60964	*The Durham Light Infantry*
		(from 4/58)

2-6-2 Class V4 (see Section 24)

3401	1700	*Bantam Cock*

ELECTRIC LOCOMOTIVES

Class EM1
(See Appendix 4)
(All named after nationalisation, by BR)

6701	26000	*Tommy (from 6/52)*
	26046	*Archimedes*

† Later rebuilt to Class K1/1 by Thompson.

*All later rebuilt to Class A2/2 4-6-2s by Thompson (501-506 numbering).

26047	*Diomedes*
26048	*Hector*
26049	*Jason*
26050	*Stentor*
26051	*Mentor*
26052	*Nestor*
26053	*Perseus*
26054	*Pluto*
26055	*Prometheus*
26056	*Triton*
26057	*Ulysses*

STEAM RAILCARS *(see Appendix 3)**

Clayton Steam Railcars

285	*Rapid*
287	*Royal Sailor*
289	*Wellington*
296	*Wonder*
2101	*Union*
2110	*Comet*
2121	*Pilot*
43302	*Chevy Chase*
43303	*Railway*
43303	*Bang Up*
43305	*Transit*

Sentinel Steam Railcars (100hp 2-cyl)

21	*Valliant*
22	*Brilliant*
26	*Tally-Ho*
29	*Rockingham*
210	*Highflyer*
212	*Eclipse*
220	*Waterwitch*
225	*True Blue*
226	*Ebor*
237	*Rodney*
238	*Yorkshire Hussar*
244	*True Briton*
250	*Rob Roy*
253	*Red Rover*
254	*Phoenix*
255	*Perseverance*
263	*North Star*
265	*Neptune*
267	*Liberty*
272	*Hero*
273	*Trafalgar*
283	*Teazle*
2135	*Integrity*

Sentinel Steam Railcars (200hp twin-engine)

220	*Defence*
246	*Royal Sovereign*
248	*Tantivy*
2281	*Old John Bull*
2283	*Old Blue*

*The final number of these railcars is shown in each case.

Sentinel Steam Railcars (100hp 6cyl)

31	*Flower of Yarrow*
32	*Fair Maid*
33	*Highland Chieftain*
34	*Tweedside*
35	*Nettle*
36	*Royal Eagle*
37	*Clydesdale*
38	*Pearl*
39	*Protector*
310	*Prince Regent*
312	*Retaliator*
313	*Banks of Don*
314	*Queen of Beauty*
2133	*Cleveland*
2136	*Hope*
2139	*Hark Forward*
2140	*Eagle*
2144	*Traveller*
2145	*Ruby*
2147	*Woodpecker*
2151	*Umpire*
2152	*Courrier*
2198	*Times*
2200	*Surprise*
2217	*Royal Charlotte*
2218	*Telegraph*
2219	*New Fly*
2231	*Swift*
2232	*Alexander*
2235	*Britannia*
2236	*British Queen*
2238	*Celerity*
2242	*Cornwallis*
2245	*Criterion*
2257	*Defiance*
2261	*Diligence*
2267	*Recovery*
2268	*Emerald*
2270	*Independent*
2271	*Industry*
2276	*North Briton*
2279	*Norfolk*
31073	*Quicksilver*
51908	*Expedition*
51909	*Waterloo*
51912	*Rising Sun*
51913	*Rival*
51914	*Royal Forrester*
43301	*Commerce*

Sentinel Steam Twin Articulated Railcar

| 2291 | *Phenomena* |

DIESEL-ELECTRIC RAILCARS
(see Appendix 3)

25	*Tyneside Venturer*
224	*Lady Hamilton*
232	*Northumbrian*

6 Preserved Locomotives

No	Name	Location	Owner	Livery
4498 (60007)	*Sir Nigel Gresley*	Steamtown, Carnforth	A4 Locomotive Society	LNER blue
60008	*Dwight D. Eisenhower*	Green Bay, Wisconsin, USA	Nat Rly Mu, Wisconsin	BR green
60009	*Union of South Africa*	Markinch, Fife	Private	BR green
60010	*Dominion of Canada*	Montreal, Canada	Montreal Rly Historical Mu	BR green
60019	*Bittern***	Stephenson Locomotive Mu	Private	LNER grey
4498 (60022)	*Mallard*	National Railway Museum	NRM, York	LNER blue
4472 (60103)	*Flying Scotsman*	Southall	Private	LNER green
4771 (60800)	*Green Arrow*	National Railway Museum	NRM, York	LNER breen
3442 (61994)	*The Great Marquess*	Severn Valley Railway	Private	LNER green
246 (62712)	*Morayshire*	Bo'ness & Kinneil Railway	Royal Scottish Museum	LNER green
4744 (69523)		Great Central Railway	The Gresley Society	LNER black

*Restored as 2509 *Silver Link*

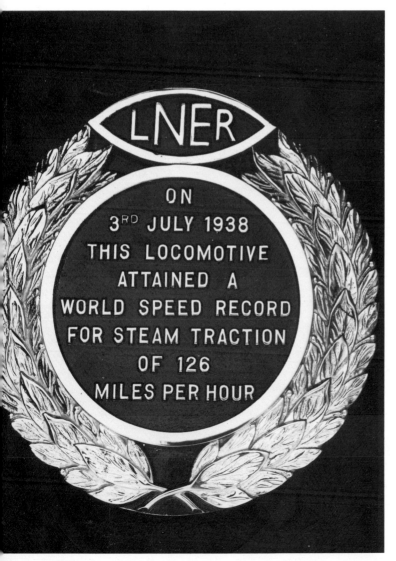

Left: The famous plaque produced for *Mallard* after it had attained a world speed record for steam traction of 126mph. These plaques, one on each side of the boiler, were added to the engine in March 1948, after nationalisation, but they carried the LNER monogram. *British Rail ER*

175

Bibliography

The following books, which were referred to in the course of compiling this pictorial history, are thoroughly recommended to the reader in search of further information about Sir Nigel Gresley and his locomotives:

Bellwood, J. and Jenkinson, D.; *Gresley and Stanier, a Centenary Tribute;* HM Stationery Office.
Brown, F.A.S.; *Nigel Gresley: Locomotive Engineer;* Ian Allan Ltd.
Brown F.A.S.; *From Stirling to Gresley, 1882-1922;* Oxford Publishing Co.
Bulleid, H.A.V.; *Master Builders of Steam;* Ian Allan Ltd.
Clay, J.F and Cliffe, J.; *The LNER 2-8-2 and 2-6-2 Classes;* Ian Allan Ltd. *The LNER 2-6-0 Classes;* Ian Allan Ltd.
Allen, G. Freeman; *Salute to the LNER,* Ian Allan Ltd.
Nock, O.S.; *The Gresley Pacifics,* (2 vols). David & Charles.
Nock O.S.; *The Locomotives of Sir Nigel Gresley,* The Railway Publishing Co.
Nock, O.S.; *LNER Steam,* David & Charles.
Prentice, K.R., and Proud, P.; *Locomotives of the LNER 1923-1937,* RCTS.

Railway Correspondence and Travel Society; *Locomotives of the LNER,* RCTS (partworks).
Reed, B.; *LNER Non-streamlined Pacifics,* (Locomotive Profiles No. 1) Profile Publications.
Reed, B and Scott, R.; *Gresley A4s,* (Locomotive Profiles No 19) Profile Publications.
Spencer, B.; *The Development of LNER Locomotives Design, 1923-1941;* (paper No 465, Institution of Locomotive Engineers, 1947).
Townend, P.N.; *Top Shed;* Ian Allan Ltd.

Additional, and valuable sources of information to the author have been:
The Gresley Observer (The Gresley Society), *The Railway Magazine, Trains Illustrated, Modern Railways, The Railway Gazette, Locomotive Magazine.*

Below: The tail end of the 11.30am 'Queen of Scots Pullman' to Edinburgh and Glasgow; leaving Kings Cross on 6 July 1948. In the background stands Class V2 2-6-2 No 915, in black livery. The silver roofs and polished handrails on the Pullman cars contrast brilliantly with the sooty atmosphere of the tunnel mouth, in a defiant blaze of postwar optimism. *C. C. B. Herbert*